Free the Mail

Free the Mail
Ending the Postal Monopoly

edited by Peter Ferrara

CATO
INSTITUTE
Washington, D.C.

Library of Congress Cataloging-in-Publication Data

Free the Mail : ending the postal monopoly / edited by Peter J. Ferrara.
   p. cm.
  Includes bibliographical references.
  ISBN 0-932790-75-5 : $25.95.—ISBN 0-932790-76-3 : $12.95
   1. United States Postal Service—Management. 2. Postal Service—
United States—Management. 3. Privatization—United States.
I. Ferrara, Peter J., 1956-
HE6371.F74   1990
383'.4973—dc20   89-71320
                                                                     CIP

Printed in the United States of America.

CATO INSTITUTE
224 Second Street SE
Washington, D.C. 20003

Contents

1. Ending the Postal Monopoly

Peter J. Ferrara

The U.S. Postal Service is a monopoly by government decree. That is the problem. The law prohibits any other firm or individual from delivering letters or other first class mail. Competing firms also cannot deliver addressed circulars, advertisements, solicitations, mass mailings, or other third class mail. Moreover, no one except the Postal Service can place anything in the mailbox of a home or business, even if the owner consents. That creates a disabling disadvantage for potential competitors in the delivery of other items, such as magazines, unaddressed third class mail, and small packages, for which private delivery is technically not prohibited. The federal government also provides cash subsidies to the Postal Service each year, which puts potential competitors at a further disadvantage.

In a society that values freedom, the prohibition on private mail delivery should seem not only anomalous but authoritarian. The decision of one individual to hire another to deliver his or her mail hardly seems to pose the kind of threat to others that should be punishable as a crime. The prohibition of private mail service deprives consumers of the freedom to choose who will deliver their mail, and it deprives entrepreneurs and their employees of the freedom to pursue economic opportunities. The policy consequently adds up to a substantial restriction on economic freedom, which in itself should be good enough reason for repeal.

The government-mandated postal monopoly also produces some rather concrete economic problems. Because the Postal Service does not face the threat of competition, it lacks incentives to control costs and maintain high quality. Instead, the Postal Service is able to overpay its bureaucracy in salary, perks, and benefits, while minimizing work obligations for each employee. The organization does not put pressure on workers to maximize effort, minimize waste

1

and costs, and produce the best service for consumers, as do organizations that must face competition every day. The Postal Service is also slow to adopt cost-saving or quality-enhancing innovations because it need not be concerned about competitors adopting such innovations first. Indeed, we do not know what startling, sweeping innovations in postal service and mail delivery might develop in a private competitive market–the very nature of the industry might be transformed.

Because of those problems, postal consumers face high and rapidly rising costs. Despite all the postal bureaucracy's talk of changes to reduce costs and improve efficiency, that same bureaucracy is now asking for a 20 percent increase in the price of a first class stamp, from 25 to 30 cents. A recent study by the Postal Service itself found that costs for routes on which services are contracted out to the private sector are about 50 percent less than the cost for the Postal Service to provide the same service directly.[1] Along with high costs, consumers suffer poor and deteriorating quality. Mail delivery is slow, unreliable, and unpredictable. Mail is lost or even discarded. Post office hours and services are inconvenient.

Leaving Behind the Pony Express

What should be most striking about the government's role in postal services today is how anachronistic it is. As Moore points out,[2] the government originally established the post office to ensure communication with the frontier in the early days of the Republic. At that time, communication technology was primitive and no other nationwide communications network existed. Given that context, we can understand how policymakers might have felt that a national postal communications network was basic infrastructure that the government should provide (though a government monopoly was probably not the wisest way of addressing the issue even at that time).

Today, however, not only national but global communication at the push of a button is commonplace. Telephones reach every nook and cranny of the nation, and some now are even portable. The nation is blanketed and bound together by radio and television,

[1] Postal Inspectors Service Study (August 1988), in letter from John Crutcher, 1989.

[2] Thomas Gale Moore, "The Federal Postal Monopoly: History, Rationale, and Future," in this book.

including endless cable channels and private transmissions. Communication today is by satellite, with receiver dishes popping up in apartment windows as well as in back yards. Computer systems are linked across the nation and around the world. They can transmit data and print out documents anywhere in an instant. Inexpensive and ubiquitous facsimile machines transmit documents anywhere in the nation in seconds at the cost of a phone call. Moreover, by waiver from the Postal Service monopoly, a number of private services will now deliver letters, documents, and packages anywhere in the nation in a matter of hours.

In this modern world, mail delivery is just another service. It is not basic infrastructure essential to binding together and unifying the nation, as bureaucrats maintain. No rationale remains for any government role in postal service, let alone a government monopoly.

The Postal Service argues that without its monopoly it would be unable to use revenues from profitable urban and commercial mail to provide service for unprofitable rural mail, leaving rural areas without service or at least without adequate service. But if the private market can deliver sugar and salt, gasoline, and clothing and furniture to rural areas, it can also deliver the mail. The private market would develop a universal mail delivery system without a government monopoly, just as it has developed universal distribution systems for food, gasoline, and consumer goods.

Indeed, many of the private postal competitors that are allowed to operate today, such as Federal Express and United Parcel Service (UPS), already deliver nationwide. They have found a strong consumer preference for services that deliver anywhere, and providing universal service is not particularly difficult or costly. Those private firms also charge standard fees nationwide; there are no extra charges for rural delivery. As Ely suggests,[3] any extra costs for rural delivery do not seem to be worth the cost and complexity of charging price differentials for them. Moreover, in an open market, as Moore suggests,[4] smaller postal firms would probably cooperate with each other to create a nationwide network for their customers as well.

[3]Bert Ely, "Privatizing the Postal Service: Why Do It; How to Do It," in this book.
[4]Moore.

3

A private competitive market would also be so much more efficient than the current monopoly Postal Service that charges for
rural delivery would probably be much less than they are now,
even without any subsidy. As indicated above, private mail delivery
can regularly cost 50 percent less than delivery by the Postal Service.
Given that cost differential, any issue of rural subsidies should be
moot.[5]

Miller ultimately calls the bluff on this key Postal Service argument.[6] If rural delivery is the concern, he suggests, why not allow
competition just on rural routes? If private delivery firms could
provide less costly or better service, rural consumers would clearly
be better off. If private firms could not do so, rural consumers could
continue to use the Postal Service and would be no worse off.

The postal monopoly today is simply special interest protectionism for the benefit of the postal bureaucracy. It allows postal bureaucrats to shower themselves with high wages, salaries, and pensions
for a minimum amount of work. It leaves them free from the competitive pressures that demand hard work, high quality, innovation, and foresight in the open marketplace. It allows them to sit
back comfortably in their effectively guaranteed, lifetime tenure.
Unfortunately, too many influential segments of our society are
blind to special interest pleading from a government bureaucracy.
Too many naively assume that public bureaucrats act in the public
interest rather than in their own personal, special interests. But as
Butler suggests,[7] the current postal monopoly cannot be considered
a public service. As long as postal service is a monopoly, it will not
be run in the interest of the public but in the interest of the postal
bureaucracy.

---

[5]Moreover, even if rural subsidies were thought necessary or desirable, providing
them by adopting a postal monopoly to overcharge for urban and commercial mail
would be grossly inefficient. The price for urban and commercial mail would not
reflect its true costs and would consequently distort the use of such mail. Moreover,
the monopoly necessary to impose such overcharges would itself naturally involve
much inefficiency and waste, as described above. Instead, the federal government
could provide explicit subsidies to a privatized postal service, and even to its new
competitors, in return for reduced rural charges. No valid justification exists, however, for taxing or overcharging urban and commercial customers to subsidize rural
customers.

[6]James C. Miller III, "Free the Mail, Part I," in this book.

[7]Stuart M. Butler, "How to Privatize the Postal Service," in this book.

Most of the chapters in this book were first given as papers at a conference on the Postal Service held by the Cato Institute in Washington, D.C., in April 1988. The authors include present and past government officials involved in postal policy and private-sector scholars and experts on the subject. Their chapters document in greater detail the economic problems that arise from the Postal Service monopoly. They also provide several different, practical proposals that would effectively revoke the monopoly, remove the system's remaining ties to the government, and ultimately leave it to compete in the open market as a private corporation. Together, these papers constitute a compelling case for reform.

The authors do not agree on the particular reforms to be adopted to address the postal monopoly problem, though they all agree that the ideal would be to eliminate the monopoly and all other Postal Service ties to the government. Their differences arise from varying views on how best to achieve or move toward that goal given practical political pressures. As Butler suggests,[8] the focus must ultimately be on developing a reform plan that has a good chance of political success.

Proposals for Reform

Based on the discussions presented here, two particular reform approaches can be developed that appear politically practical and capable of achieving the ultimate goals. The first is a gradual approach that would repeal the postal monopoly and privatize the system step by step. In 1971 the U.S. government's postal system was transformed into a semiprivate corporation called the U.S. Postal Service, which makes the gradual approach more feasible. This corporation owns all postal service buildings and property and officially hires all postal employees. Its board of directors, called the Board of Governors, is appointed by the president with Senate approval. The board then selects the postmaster general, who serves as chief executive officer of the corporation. The president also appoints a Postal Rate Commission, which must approve changes in postal fees and services.

The first step in the gradual approach would be to repeal the monopoly for third class mail, which as noted above includes

[8]Ibid.

5

addressed advertisements, solicitations, and mass mailings. Senders of such mail would then be free to choose private firms to deliver it instead of the Postal Service. Achieving this first step is especially promising because the businesses that conduct such mailings have become outraged by the Postal Service's rapidly rising costs and poor service. They now favor repeal of the third class mail monopoly and would work hard for it. At the same time, the public is not concerned about such mail and would not be alarmed by reforms that applied to it. Furthermore, that change would not require legislation. The Postal Service has the authority to implement it by regulation. A president who favored such reform could appoint a Postal Service Board of Governors willing to carry it out. Of course, the change could always be made by statute, which would make it harder to reverse.

Repeal of the monopoly on third class mail would create momentum for further reform. As private third class mail firms provided better service at lower cost, the public would see that a private competitive market in mail delivery could work well. The next step would be to remove the remaining Postal Service monopoly on the mailbox. Private companies would be allowed to place all the types of mail they are allowed to deliver under current law directly in residential and business mailboxes: second class mail, which includes magazines and newspapers; both addressed and unaddressed third class mail (addressed third class mail should be allowed to go into mailboxes under step one); and fourth class mail, which includes packages, books, films, and other material. The postal Board of Governors, again, currently has the authority to adopt such a change.

The postal unions will no doubt try to scare the public with phony arguments that private mail delivery firms cannot be trusted with access to mailboxes. They will suggest that broader access would undermine the security of mailboxes and create an opportunity for mail theft. But where private competitors, such as Federal Express and UPS, are allowed to operate today, the public uses them far more heavily than the Postal Service, which indicates that the public is not concerned about the security and trustworthiness of private mail delivery. Indeed, many businesses prefer the private competitors precisely because they are more secure and reliable than the Postal Service. Private mail companies know that security breaches

6

in their service would lead to the demise of their business, and consequently they strenuously guard against any such breach. Absent a concrete problem, private mail security is unlikely to be a major public issue that will sway many votes. The mailbox monopoly could also be broken by statute, though the legislative effort would provide the postal unions greater opportunity to stir up trouble. Once that change was achieved, only the monopoly of first class mail would remain intact.

The next step would be to repeal government subsidies for the Postal Service. The major one is an annual subsidy of about $2.5 billion for employee pensions and retirement health benefits. The Postal Service also can borrow from the U.S. Treasury. Phasing out those two subsidies would require legislation. The federal government also provides the Postal Service about $700 million per year to compensate it for reduced rates required by law for mail sent by nonprofit charitable organizations. Since this compensates the Postal Service for a legally mandated reduced rate, it is a subsidy not to the Postal Service but to nonprofit charities. Attempts to abolish it would allow postal unions to enlist numerous nonprofit charities in opposition to the privatization reforms. Perhaps waiting until after privatization was complete to reconsider this subsidy would be wiser.

The Postal Rate Commission's regulatory authority over charges and services for second, third, and fourth class mail could also be revoked when subsidies to the Postal Service are eliminated. With the postal monopoly of those categories abolished, and no remaining subsidy for the Postal Service, the government would no longer have any reason to maintain such regulation. The Postal Service would then be free to set its own rates and services to meet the competition. That change would again require legislation.

Finally, efforts could be made to chip away at the remaining first class mail monopoly. Private firms could be allowed to deliver first class mail within and into rural areas. If the rationale for the monopoly is concern that the private market would not deliver to such areas, then surely there can be no objection to letting the private sector try to do so. As suggested above, if private firms could provide better or less expensive services, rural areas would benefit, and if the private firms could not, the rural areas could continue to use the Postal Service. Private firms could also be

7

allowed to deliver first class mail between businesses. The business community would probably strongly favor such a change because private mail delivery would be more reliable and efficient. The general public would probably not be concerned about what happened to first class business mail, particularly since such mail does not generate any significant subsidies for residential mail.

Those changes would ultimately leave a comparatively narrow postal monopoly. At the same time, the public would see a flowering of superior, competitive, private mail delivery services and become increasingly familiar with using them. In that environment, the predicted dire consequences of eliminating the remaining monopoly would be implausible and the benefits of doing so far more obvious. Those factors might combine to make elimination of the remaining monopoly politically feasible.

The second possible approach to reform would be to eliminate the postal monopoly and privatize the Postal Service all at once in one carefully crafted package. That approach would be based on the now classic formula of buying off the vested interests opposing a privatization plan with some of the benefits that would result from its implementation. In our case, the vested interests would be the Postal Service workers and management. To maximize the possible success of this approach, the privatization plan should be made far more attractive to those workers and management than anyone has yet proposed.

The federal government could issue stock to current workers and management for the entire value and ownership stake of the Postal Service. That would grant them outright ownership of a multibillion dollar enterprise. Included in the kitty would be ownership of thousands of real estate properties across the country currently held by the Postal Service for post offices, warehouses, and other functions. Much of that property is underutilized and could be immediately sold off, with the profits going to the new worker and management owners. The federal government could also retain responsibility for current unfunded pension and retirement health benefit liabilities, while the Postal Service assumed responsibility for funding all future benefits. The Postal Service would no longer borrow from the federal government, but it would continue to receive federal compensation for reduced-rate charity mailing as long as such reduced rates were required. The Postal Rate Commission would be abolished, and the Postal Service would have complete control over its rates and services. The Board of Governors would be elected by the stockholders rather than appointed by the president. At the same time, the postal monopoly on all classes of mail would be entirely abolished. Private competitors would have the same access to mailboxes as the Postal Service.

The value of the stock provided to each employee under this plan would be tens of thousands of dollars. Top Postal Service managers who assumed entrepreneurial responsibility would be free of federal salary restrictions that keep their incomes far below private-sector levels for executives of a major enterprise. Postal management would also be free to run the Postal Service as a major private-sector business, growing with the numerous economic opportunities that would be open to it. Those advantages might be sufficient to gain the support of Postal Service workers and management for the privatization plan. If that support were obtained, the plan would be assured of enactment. While in theory the federal government under this plan would be losing the substantial sums it would receive from an outright sale of the Postal Service to the public, such profits are a mirage—proponents of such a sale would be unlikely to overcome the opposition of the entrenched postal bureaucracy. That opposition can be overcome politically only by effectively distributing the value of the institution to postal workers and management and thereby winning their support. The benefits to the public and the economy of privatization alone make it worthwhile to pursue such a plan. Moreover, the Postal Service would become a federal taxpayer, and the cost of current federal subsidies to the Postal Service would be eliminated over time.

Either of the two approaches would achieve the ultimate goals of abolishing the postal monopoly and privatizing the Postal Service. The choice between them hinges on which is the most likely to win political approval. If both approaches seemed likely to succeed, the quickest method would be the best. The two approaches, in fact, are not mutually exclusive. The gradual approach could be introduced first, and then the one-shot package could be adopted as soon as it was feasible. Progress on the gradual approach would probably enhance the political prospects for the more direct approach.

Whatever the precise approach taken, those who have the common interest clearly in view must favor repeal of the postal monopoly. Fighting government monopolies has a long and hallowed tradition in Anglo-American history. Today's struggle to free the mail is a continuation of that honored tradition.

2. The Slow Death of the U.S. Postal Service

James Bovard

Mail service in the United States is getting slower, more expensive, and less reliable. First class mail moves 15 percent slower than it did in 1969. The cost of first class postage is rising twice as fast as inflation. According to the U.S. Postal Service's own figures, postal worker productivity has declined during the 1980s.

The Postal Service is misleading the American public on the quality of mail service it provides. Post office hours have been slashed, mail has been intentionally slowed down, and millions of Americans have been denied home mail delivery. In some cities, post offices are opening an hour later in the morning and the last mail pickup of the day is now at 4 o'clock in the afternoon. The Postal Service would like to do even more: In 1986, for example, Postmaster General Albert Casey advocated abolishing Monday mail deliveries and abolishing standards for two-day delivery of first class mail.[1]

The history of the Postal Service in the 1980s is largely a history of boondoggles. From the electronic mail system that squandered tens of millions of dollars, to the 21 massive bulk mail centers that helped sink the parcel post business, to the nine-digit ZIP Code that is enduring a lingering death, to the rapidly dying Express Mail, the Postal Service has repeatedly staked its prestige on programs that have brought it nothing but embarrassment.

There have been five postmasters general in less than five years, yet there has been a continued decline in service. Again and again, the public has heard promises of a "new Postal Service." But, even

The author, an associate policy analyst of the Cato Institute, has written widely on the U.S. Postal Service for the *Wall Street Journal* and the *New York Times*.

[1]James Bovard "Prepare for Mail Talks, Parcel Out Work," *Wall Street Journal*, January 9, 1987.

with the big rate increase, the Postal Service is expected to lose over a billion dollars a year.

The Postal Service, like almost every monopoly in history, treats its customers with disdain. A recent White House–Congress budget agreement required the Postal Service to save $116 million during the 1988 fiscal year, which represents roughly 0.5 percent of the Postal Service's annual budget. According to a Postal Service audit, the Postal Service loses $636 million a year just from postal carriers wasting an hour and a half a day. However, instead of improving management and reducing waste, the Postal Service slashed its window hours and eliminated mail processing on Sunday. And despite written promises to the contrary, it began closing post offices on Saturday in Detroit, Cincinnati, Philadelphia, Atlanta, Los Angeles, New York, and smaller cities.[2]

Mail service in the United States is slow and unreliable because the government has a monopoly. As long as the Postal Service has no competition, it will have little or no incentive to treat its customers with the respect they receive elsewhere in a competitive economy.

With over 800,000 employees, the Postal Service is the United States' largest employer. It added more new employees—150,000—during the Reagan years than were cut by all other federal agencies to reduce federal employment. However, the more workers the Postal Service has hired, the worse service has become, and the more incorrigible the system appears to be. On top of this, according to Postal Rate Commissioner John Crutcher, U.S. postal workers are "the highest paid semiskilled workers in the world."[3] The average annual remuneration—including overtime pay and benefits—is now $38,751 per worker.[4]

The Great American Mail Slowdown

A 1987 Postal Service poster proclaimed, "The new Postal Service. We're changing. We move mountains of mail for you . . . Amazingly accurate . . . Amazingly fast . . . We're delivering the mail

[2]Judith Havemann, "Postal Service Allows Some Saturday Closings," *Washington Post*, March 27, 1988.

[3]John Crutcher, speech delivered to the Commonwealth Club of California, San Francisco, August 26, 1983.

[4]Data in "National Payroll Hour Summary Report" and "National Consolidated Trial Balance," U.S. Postal Service, accounting period 4, 1988.

faster than ever." Dishonesty becomes almost inevitable in an incompetent bureaucracy trying to hide its failures from the public.

The Postal Service has always had a generous amount of contempt for its customers. In the mid-1970s it seriously considered saving money by educating its customers not to expect "prompt service." A 1974 classified postal audit revealed that the Postal Service damaged half the packages marked "fragile" that it carried.[5] Postmaster General Elmer Klassen conceded in 1973 that the Postal Service damaged five times as many packages as United Parcel Service.[6] Clerks in the New York Post Office were formally told not to throw fragile packages more than five feet.[7]

The Postal Service may soon have to file environmental impact statements for all the mail it is dumping in America's trash boxes and dumpsters. For example, a Rhode Island carrier was arrested after 94,000 letters were found buried in his backyard.[8] A 1987 survey by Doubleday and Company found that up to 14 percent of bulk business mail was either thrown away or lost.[9] One Arlington, Virginia, postal clerk told a customer, "We don't have room for the junk mail—so we've been throwing it out."[10] In 1987, 1,315 postal workers were fired for theft or mistreatment of mail, or both.[11] A Postal Inspection Service audit found properly addressed mail dumped in the trash at 76 percent of the post offices it visited.[12] A survey by Doubleday found that up to 14 percent of properly addressed third class mail vanished in the postal labyrinth.[13] The throwing away of mail has become so pervasive that postal inspectors have notified employees that it is bad for the Postal Service's business.[14]

[5]*Washington Post*, June 10, 1974. This and most newspaper items cited in this study are available in the Postal Service's *Daily News Digest*.

[6]John Haldi, *Postal Monopoly: An Assessment of the Private Express Statutes* (Washington: American Enterprise Institute, 1974), p. 47.

[7]*Washington Post*, June 11, 1974.

[8]James Bovard, "Enough Fourth-Class Service on Third-Class Mail," *New York Times*, June 9, 1987.

[9]*Business Mailers Review*, November 9, 1987.

[10]Ibid.

[11]*Washington Times*, January 5, 1988.

[12]*Direct Mail News*, March 1, 1988.

[13]*Third Class Mail Association Bulletin*, February 19, 1988.

[14]Bovard, "Prepare for Mail Talks."

The *Charlotte Observer* recently surveyed Charlotte mailers and found 14 of 20 "had experienced delayed deliveries, disappearing mail and harassment by postal workers when they objected to poor service."[15] According to Ivan Mothershead, a North Carolina state representative, "When you complain, you get worse service. If they want to hassle you, they hold up your mail and say it's not right." The situation became so bad that mail processing director W. H. Ireland, Jr., openly accused postal workers "of sabotaging deliveries and creating delays to collect overtime pay."[16]

The mail that the Postal Service does not throw away is getting delivered much slower now than in previous decades, and it isn't just the public that worries about slow service—so do the postal workers themselves. Each week, postal paychecks are mailed from Minnesota to post offices around the country. When the checks were very late in getting to the post office in Radford, Virginia, one of the affected workers there publicly said he wanted the next postal union contract to specify that postal paychecks be carried by UPS to ensure that they arrive on time.[17] Postmasters have been complaining lately because the *National Association of Postmasters Magazine* keeps arriving late.[18]

When the chairman of the Federal Trade Commission made a speech criticizing the postal monopoly, Postmaster General Preston Robert Tisch wrote an indignant response. Because Tisch's response was so important, he sent it by private courier.[19] UPS employee Thomas J. Vandevela commented in a San Diego newspaper, "At Christmas time, it is common to see postal employees in uniform using UPS. Let me ask the readers—'Has anyone ever seen a UPS driver trying to mail a package at the Post Office?' "[20]

When Rep. Bill Green did a survey of first class mail delivery in Manhattan, he found that 32 percent of the mail was delivered late by USPS standards.[21] A Washington television station did a survey

[15]Ed Martin, "Post Office Sometimes Doesn't Deliver, Critics Say," *Charlotte Observer*, January 10, 1988.

[16]Ibid.

[17]Editorial, *Washington Times*, August 27, 1987.

[18]*Business Mailers Review*, February 9, 1987.

[19]"Washington Wire," *Wall Street Journal*, June 19, 1987, p. 1.

[20]*San Diego Union*, January 7, 1988.

[21]Bovard, "Prepare for Mail Talks."

and found that 24 percent of the mail in the Washington area was delivered late.[22] A Postal Service survey found that 83 percent of non-carrier-route-sorted third class mail was late.[23] A 1987 Red Tag Mail Association survey found that 69 percent of second class mail was delivered late.[24]

Nevertheless, the Postal Service continues to claim that it is delivering 95 percent of first class mail in metropolitan areas the next day. This is postal fraud—nothing more, nothing less. If an advertiser made the same claims about a product sold through the mails, the postal inspectors would try to shut down his business.

The Postal Service measures mail delivery speed with its Origin-Destination Information System (ODIS). But ODIS is designed to provide grossly biased information. It does not measure actual delivery; rather, it measures only when a letter leaves the originating postal facility and arrives at the final postal facility. ODIS is designed to make mail service appear far speedier than it actually is. This system judges not whether the Postal Service provides good service to the public, but whether it goes through the bureaucratic motions.

Even using ODIS, some postal officials still feel compelled to manipulate the statistics. A 1987 Postal Inspection Service survey, for example, found widespread cheating by local post offices.[25] Cleveland clerks told inspectors of "subtle forms of intimidation" from management to get good results.[26] As *Business Mailers Review* noted, "Two postmasters, in a candid moment, said that if ODIS tests were conducted by private auditors, the percentage of letters reported to be delivered on time would drop by as much as 20 points."[27] Employees are "under substantial pressure to come up with right numbers,"[28] and some have been bumped out of their jobs because they refused to cheat on the mail delivery tests. In

[22]Station WJLA (channel 7) news program broadcast on December 30, 1987; transcript in Postal Service's press clip collection.

[23]Cited in *Business Mailers Review*, December 13, 1986; also in Bovard, "Prepare for Mail Talks."

[24]Red Tag Mail Association, *Consolidated Postal Delivery Analysis*.

[25]*Business Mailers Review*, July 13, 1987.

[26]Ibid.

[27]Ibid.

[28]Ibid.

15

Atlanta, almost a dozen supervisors were demoted or suspended after they were caught finagling with mail test results. As Van Seagraves notes, "Postmasters get bonuses for good numbers. Because they know the day before the routes that will be sampled, there is an opportunity to shade results."[29]

The Postal Service takes its standards very seriously. The service has always had trouble moving the mail on time. In 1987 it came up with a brilliant innovation: it changed the final mail pickup time in scores of cities from 5 p.m. or later to 4 p.m. In Washington, mail pickups were moved back from 6:30 p.m. to 5 p.m. (although public pressure did force the Postal Service to roll back the pickup time to 6:30 at a few places in Washington). The *Washington Post* complimented the Postal Service on this move: "If there's not enough time to get something done on time, drop the task and keep your standards high."[30]

Even the Postal Service's rigged ODIS measurement shows that first class mail service is getting ever slower. In 1969 the average first class letter required 1.50 days to be delivered; by 1982 this average had increased to 1.65 days. By late 1987 the average time required for delivery had slipped to 1.72 days.[31]

The Postal Service claims a 97 percent success rate with its Express Mail service. However, the ODIS method of judging performance is especially absurd when applied to a courier letter. Over half of the Express Mail I receive is late. I once stopped a carrier who was bringing me a late Express Mail letter and asked him how many were late; he shuffled through his clips, smiled, and said, "About 70 percent."

The Postal Service is paranoid about criticisms of its performance. As the Orange County *Register* reported, a sales firm in New Jersey adopted the humorous slogan, "Service with a snarl. High prices— Rotten delivery. Stupid salesmen," and put it on the firm's postage meter. Postal Service inspectors, concerned that people would think that the new slogan was theirs, forced the firm to change its slogan.

[29]Ibid.

[30]*Washington Post* editorial, cited in Robert Walters, "Delivering Doctored Numbers?" *Washington Times*, July 31, 1987.

[31]U.S. Postal Service, *Origin-Destination Quarterly Statistical Report, FY 1988, Quarter 1*, p. 7.

Saving Money by Abolishing Service

When the Postal Service talks of saving money, the first thing it thinks of is cutting service. This is what happens when an organization has captive customers.

In Albany, New York, the Postal Service canceled Saturday mail deliveries around Christmas and New Year's to save money.[32] Across the United States, in response to a tiny, congressionally mandated budget cut, post offices reduced window hours by 10 percent. Different post offices close their doors at different times, so no one can be sure when any given post office will be open. Some post offices, in fact, now close during lunch hours, a particular problem for working people who need to pick up a package during the day.

In the Albany area, postal spokesman James R. Hodgins said, "We named 1988 as 'the year of the customer.' This [budget cut] is really going to cut into that."[33] It only took a revenue reduction of 0.5 percent to persuade the Postal Service to dramatically reduce customer service. Private firms deal with much larger fluctuations in revenue all the time without deciding to take it out of their customers' hides.

In northern Virginia, the population is rising rapidly and mail service is notoriously poor. Fran Ford, a postal spokesperson, reassured the *Washington Post* that the situation was not so bad, insisting that all first class mail was being delivered to people's homes by 6 p.m.[34] A few decades ago, America enjoyed twice-a-day mail delivery; now, the Postal Service thinks it does well enough if the mail arrives before the moon rises.

The Cluster Box Program is one of the Postal Service's great hopes for saving money in the future. It is based on the assumption that the Postal Service could save money if it stopped carrying the mail to people's homes. Mail delivery to residential doorsteps was abolished in 1978 for new homes, and is gradually being phased out for older homes. Instead, the Postal Service is imposing a new mail delivery system under which mail is delivered to central locations—cluster boxes—and mail recipients have to travel a half-mile

[32]*Albany Times-Union*, December 24, 1987.
[33]Ibid.
[34]*Washington Post*, February 5, 1988.

17

or more to get their mail. What is more, the Postal Service will prosecute anyone who delivers mail to people's doors.

In Maryville, Tennessee, residents in one neighborhood who refused to surrender home delivery and sign up for cluster boxes were told that their mail would be temporarily held at the post office, where they could go and collect it.[35] As Postmaster J. N. Campbell of Virginia Beach, Virginia, declared, "The old days of mail being taken to your home are coming to an end. Efficiency is first in our minds."[36]

Assistant Postmaster General Frank Johnson defends the postal monopoly, claiming that allowing private competition would "endanger the principle of universal service."[37] However, to safeguard the "principle of universal service," the Postal Service is providing less and less service to everyone.

Where Have All the Billions Gone?

Why are postal rates rising so much faster than inflation, at the same time that mail service appears rapidly heading for extinction?

The Postal Service bought a jet, which provided very pleasant flights for postmasters general and their wives on weekend trips from Washington to Chicago or New York.[38] (Pressure from Rep. Glenn English forced the Postal Service to relinquish the plane.) In Hawaii, postal workers spent their time giving workshops on how to write love letters.[39]

A Postal Service audit found that the typical letter carrier wastes an hour and a half a day, which costs the Postal Service more than $636 million a year.[40] The average UPS employee probably moves three times as fast as the average postal worker, and the average Federal Express worker moves twice as fast. Postal workers move slower than private carriers because postal workers have different

[35]House Government Operations Committee, *Postal Service Moves Toward Centralized Mail Delivery*, March 15, 1983, p. 48.

[36]Norfolk *Virginian-Pilot*, December 19, 1983.

[37]*New York Times*, letter to the editor, June 19, 1987.

[38]Marianne Szegedy-Maszak, "The Twenty-Five Cent Stamp," *Washington Monthly*, November 1987, p. 41.

[39]*Windward Sun Press* (Kareohe, Hawaii), February 4, 1988.

[40]*Business Mailers Review*, January 27, 1986.

incentives—and de facto guaranteed lifetime jobs. "Fast enough for government work" is the reigning sentiment.

Postal productivity standards are abysmal. Private letter-sorting bureaus can sort the mail for less than half what it costs the Postal Service to do so. It costs the Postal Service roughly five cents to sort each letter down to the ZIP Code. The Postal Service offers a four-cent discount for presorting down to the ZIP Code, and many corporations contract with private sorting bureaus and split the four-cent difference. The vast majority of mail volume growth in recent years has stemmed from presorted mail.

Postal Service clerks have a far lower productivity rate than clerks in efficient private stores. McDonald's clerks getting $4 an hour are more efficient—and friendlier—than postal clerks getting $15 an hour. A new computer program allows clerks in private post office services to instantly figure the weight and rate for packages, and to tell the customer the comparative cost of sending a package by the Postal Service, UPS, and Roadway Package System. Yet many federal post offices still plod along with manual scales. Given the Postal Service's high wages, new computers could pay for themselves very quickly. But because the Postal Service has no competition, it has no incentive to innovate.

According to Ruth Peters of the Postal Board of Governors, "Our productivity is quite low at this moment."[41] According to Postal Rate Commissioner Patti Birge Tyson, "Postal productivity appears to be falling—in spite of a $1 billion expenditure on letter-processing automation over the last few years and additional billions on facilities."[42]

One postal worker recently commented, "Workers that don't produce aren't corrected. In this past Christmas season workers were given four hours overtime every day and they don't throw enough mail to justify one hour. No supervisor jumps these lazy bums and tells them to either produce or go home. . . . There is no accountability, no one cares."[43] Several former mail carriers told me they were "warned" after their first few days on the job that they should stop hustling and making everyone else look bad.

[41]Ruth Peters, Postal Board of Governors, interview with author, March 15, 1988.

[42]Patti Birge Tyson, speech delivered to the Direct Mail Association, Washington, May 15, 1987.

[43]*Business Mailers Review*, January 11, 1988.

The Postal Service grossly mismanages its labor costs. It hires temporary workers to do the same work as permanent workers and pays the temporaries only $5.35 an hour—less than a third of the average pay for permanent workers. This is clear proof that the Postal Service overpays most of its workers.

The Postal Service wanted to increase the number of so-called casual workers in the last labor negotiations from 5 percent to 10 percent of the total work force, but the unions naturally didn't like the idea, so management abandoned it.

Saving money seems to be the last thing that interests the Postal Service. It pays its own janitors $10.89 per hour, while private janitors who mop Postal Service floors receive an average of only $4.44 per hour, according to the General Accounting Office.[44] The Postal Service contracts out some of its rural letter routes to private star route carriers, and thereby saves up to 60 percent of the cost of carrying the mail itself.[45]

Deputy Postmaster General Jackie Strange said in 1986 that the Postal Service planned to save money by contracting out. However, the only major privatization effort has been to contract out the repair of old mailbags.[46] An official Postal Service magazine recently included an article entitled "Privatization: A Clear and Present Danger?" featuring a full-page picture of the shadow of an ax hanging over the Postal Service logo.[47] The Postal Service prefers to keep all its business in its own hands, even though it would be far cheaper to divide the labor with private companies.

Keeping a Grip on Third Class Mail

A survey by the American Newspaper Publishers Association found that third class mail receives almost the same quality of service as first class mail.[48] Although the Postal Service denies that it is providing a better deal to third class mailers than to first class mailers, it charges first class mailers six times more for the same

---

[44]General Accounting Office, *The Postal Service Can Substantially Reduce Its Cleaning Costs* (Washington, 1982), p. i.

[45]*Wall Street Journal*, August 3, 1984.

[46]Bovard, "Prepare for Mail Talks."

[47]Ibid.

[48]Bovard, "Enough Fourth-Class Service on Third-Class Mail."

three-ounce letter. With the new rates, first class mailers will pay only five times as much.

Many local post offices provide red carpet service to junk mailers, often at the expense of first class mail. In Michigan a regional Postal Service headquarters issued an order to local post offices to provide first class service to ADVO's mail (ADVO is one of the largest third class mailers).[49]

The Postal Service's total volume of first class mail exceeds its total volume of third class mail, but a large share of first class mail is delivered to post office boxes, mostly for large businesses such as American Express and utility companies. Postal carriers never touch this mail. Almost all third class mail, on the other hand, goes to private households. As most citizens recognize, they receive more junk mail than first class mail. The Postal Service's own testimony at rate case hearings stated that it spends 25 percent more money to stuff third class letters into residential mail boxes than it spends to deliver first class letters.[50]

Third class mail is rapidly turning postal carriers into packhorses. The average third class letter weighs three and a half times as much as the average first class letter. According to the Postal Service's 1986 annual report, the total weight of third class mail was more than double that of first class mail—6.5 billion pounds versus 2.8 billion pounds.

Even though the Postal Service is having great difficulty with the current volume of third class mail, it has repeatedly tried to drive private advertising delivery services out of business. As George Johnson of Direct Market Media of Cambridge, Minnesota, told the Postal Rate Commission: "Between 1978 and 1988, first class carrier route rates increased 53.8 percent while third class carrier route rates increased only 9.75 percent."[51] The Postal Service sets its rates to take the profits from the classes of mail where it has a monopoly to underwrite the service in classes where it faces competition.

The Postal Service still claims a monopoly on third class mail that carries an address label. This is an absurd situation. A newspaper

[49]Ken Bradstreet, vice president, Advertisers Postal Service Corp., interview with author.

[50]Testimony of Peter Hume, "Postal Rate and Fee Changes," Docket No. R87-1 U.S. Postal Rate Commission, May 14, 1987, p. 27.

[51]Testimony of George Johnson, ibid., September 14, 1987.

carrier can deliver a copy of, say, the *Wall Street Journal* with an address label featuring a customer's name and address, but K-Mart is prohibited by law from leaving a flier with an address label attached to the same customer's door. A newspaper with an address label is still a newspaper; an advertising circular with an address label is a letter, and the rightful domain of the Postal Service. The reason for the distinction is that newspapers have more clout than advertisers. As someone once said, "Never argue with someone who buys newsprint by the ton."

The Postal Service versus the Competition

Greed is the core of the postal problem. Although the Postal Service does a poor job of delivering mail, it strongly objects to any other organization delivering mail.

For 200 years, the Postal Service has played a game of catch-up with its illegal competition. It has never worried about serving its customers until after some other entity has come along and served them better.

The Postal Service has a long history of trying to squash its competition. It has harassed both UPS and Federal Express. When Federal Express was new, postal inspectors would watch for Federal Express invoices in the mail, and then visit their recipients and threaten to sue them unless they gave their business to Express Mail instead.[52]

The worse service becomes, the more anxious the Postal Service is to throttle the competition. Many corporations have long been frustrated by the Postal Service's slow mail service to Europe. As a result, private remail services sprang up that collected letters in the United States and sent them directly to foreign countries to expedite delivery. Postal Service lawyers attempted to expand the definition of monopoly to prohibit international remail, but the White House spiked the Postal Service's ambition.[53]

All of the actions taken by the Postal Service against its competitors have been justified by the service's belief that its duty is to preserve postal revenues. However, the more money the service has taken in, the worse service it has given.

[52]House Post Office and Civil Service Committee, *Hearings on the Private Express Statutes*, May 3, 1979, p. 40.

[53]James Bovard, *Wall Street Journal*, June 20, 1985.

In the areas where the Postal Service faces competition, it has been thoroughly unsuccessful. The Postal Service spent over $1 billion on new bulk mail handling centers in the 1970s, for instance, but the new centers were a disaster. The Postal Service now carries less than 10 percent of all parcels shipped by the public.[54] Postal Service economist George S. Tolley told the Postal Rate Commission, "The real price (adjusted for inflation) of UPS service decreased 6.2 percent between 1981 and 1986."[55]

The story is the same for Express Mail. Even the federal government uses a private courier—DHL—instead of the U.S. Postal Service for its express mail needs. The Postal Service's share of overnight-delivery mail has plummeted from 20 percent to less than 10 percent in the last three years. Yet the Postal Service continues with a lavish advertising campaign promoting Express Mail, largely because Express Mail is good for its image.

The Postal Service is battling private third class mail delivery services in many parts of the United States. Private mail delivery services now employ over 100,000 full- and part-time workers, according to George Johnson, who was a spokesperson (along with Ken Bradstreet) for the Association of Private Postal Systems, Inc., in the last postal rate case.[56]

Private advertising deliverers are dancing circles around the Postal Service carriers. Ken Bradstreet, of Advertisers Postal Service Corp. in Gaylord, Michigan, reports, "The Postal Service carriers fight over giving us their information on their route first, so that we can take some of their junk mail off their backs." One Midwestern private deliverer reported that postal carriers would trade their route maps for six-packs of beer.[57] On the other hand, some postal carriers did not want private competition on their routes, and would drive wildly to try to evade private carriers who were following them to make maps of their routes. One postal carrier in northern Michigan got so flustered that he crashed his jeep in a ditch. The APPS employee offered to help him out of the ditch, but the postal

---

[54]*Business Mailers Review*, June 29, 1987.

[55]Ibid.

[56]George Johnson, interview with author, February 5, 1988.

[57]Anonymous private deliverer, interview with author, February 5, 1988. This private deliverer requested anonymity because of fear of Postal Service retaliation.

carrier threatened to bash his competitor with a shovel if he came near the jeep.[58]

The Postal Service inhibits private delivery services by effectively nationalizing every postbox in the country. Currently, it is a federal crime for a local church to put its weekly flier in anyone's mailbox. The Postal Service claims it must nationalize our mailboxes to protect us against abuses. But this should be a choice left up to owners, not regulators. This rule is the Postal Service's last line of defense against competition.

The Postal Service also has an expansive definition of mailbox. Private deliverers have been told that the monopoly on a mailbox extends to a three-foot radius around the mailbox. In apartment buildings, the Postal Service claims a monopoly on the bins below mailboxes, the floor around mailboxes, and even tables in the lobby near mailboxes. One western private deliverer alleged that after his workers hung polyethylene bags of advertisements on people's doorknobs, Postal Service carriers would remove the bags and throw them on the ground.[59]

Businesses that have used private delivery services to distribute their ads have been called by local postal officials and informed that they have violated the private express statutes and owe heavy fines. This is purely an intimidation tactic. The advertisements are often not even left in a mailbox. Furthermore, the private carrier, not the advertiser, is liable for any private express statute violation. By calling the advertiser, the Postal Service tries to frighten the company into giving its business to the Postal Service instead of the private deliverer.[60]

Why a Monopoly?

A 1976 *New Yorker* cartoon expressed what could be the Postal Service's new motto: "Neither lethargy, indifference, nor the general collapse of standards will prevent these couriers from eventually delivering some of your mail."[61] The Postal Service has a

[58]Ken Bradstreet, interview with author, February 5, 1988.

[59]Anonymous private deliverer, interview with author, February 6, 1988. This deliverer also requested anonymity out of fear of Postal Service retaliation.

[60]Various members of Association of Private Postal Systems, Inc., interviews with author, February 5–6, 1988.

[61]Reprinted in *New York Times*, January 31, 1988.

monopoly so that it can be a "public service," but its very monopoly status destroys its incentive to serve the public. The Postal Service's standard for mail delivery appears to be to provide the minimal service short of provoking a public riot or cessation of the postal monopoly.

Not only does the Postal Service have the right to provide lousy service, but it has the power to prevent anyone else from providing good service. The essence of the Postal Service is that no one else is allowed to carry the mail, and the service itself will provide as little mail service as possible. "The customer be damned" has always been the natural result of the postal monopoly.

America's postal system is based on the idea that it is better to trust a public monopoly to provide service out of its own sense of obligation than to trust companies to provide good service out of sheer necessity—that an organization is more likely to serve the public when it has no competition and a guaranteed income than when it must fight for its customers. Postal Service officials continue proclaiming they provide a public service, even as they repeatedly slash service to the public.

The Postal Service is bragging that it has not lost as much money in the 1980s as it lost in the 1970s, and offers this as proof that it is better managed now. However, the fact that a monopoly makes a profit or a loss is only a measure of how much money it can extort from its customers. Postal Service revenues are healthy only in the classes of mail in which it faces no competition. If the Postal Service charged 50 cents for a first class stamp, spent $500 million a year prosecuting private delivery services, and showed a $2 billion profit, this would not be proof of business acumen. What business-man could not make a profit if he had the entire force of the federal government and the federal courts behind him?

The postal rate-making system seems to be based on the idea that the public is obliged to pay for unlimited postal inefficiencies, for unlimited waste of time by postal employees, and for an unlimited number of boondoggles in return for minimal mail service. Postal Rate Commissioner John Crutcher has fought a valiant fight throughout the 1980s, raising questions about the Postal Service's waste, fraud, and abuse, but little has changed.

The U.S. postal system is increasingly designed to serve only postal management and postal unions. In 1971, one federal district court prohibited a private firm from carrying Christmas cards in Oklahoma on the grounds that the plaintiff, a postal employees union, suffered "significant loss of work time, overtime, employment benefits . . . and morale." The court ruled that the public should suffer bad mail service so as not to adversely affect postal workers' morale.[62]

It is easier for the Postal Service to slash service to its customers than to fight its own unions. It is easier to make customers wait for opening hours than to efficiently manage its own work force. The Postal Service has always followed the path of least resistance, and that has always meant higher wages for its employees and less service for the public.

The Postal Service uses its monopoly on mail service to justify providing less and less service to citizens each year. Every reduction in service is a confession of incompetence. The Postal Service did not take any polls before it reduced its post office opening hours by 10 percent; it just took the path of least resistance. If the Postal Service slashed office opening hours by 10 percent in response to a budget cut of 0.5 percent, would post offices be closed permanently in response to a 5 percent budget cut?

The Postal Service claims a natural monopoly and then cuts back service to its customers and calls in its lawyers to prevent any private company from filling the gap. The postal monopoly assumes that mail service must be treated as a welfare item, and that people are greedy to think that their mail should be delivered quickly, or to their doorstep, or that the Postal Service should not lose more than 5 percent of the letters. Because mail service is so important, the public is supposed to get by with less and less of it each year—and should be grateful for whatever the government deigns to give them.

How to End the Postal Monopoly

There will be no meaningful reform as long as the Postal Service still has the power to outlaw its competition. Under five postmasters general in less than five years, service has continued to deteriorate. The Postal Service announces a new panacea every year or two,

---

[62]James Bovard, "Postal Monopoly Only Fuels Inflation," *Chicago Tribune*, April 28, 1980.

and then, after another salvation scheme bites the dust, announces a new one. But nothing will change as long as the Postal Service has so little competition for first class mail.

An excellent approach to undermining the monopoly would be to end the postal monopoly on home delivery of junk mail. Allowing private carriers to handle third class mail would save the Postal Service from collapsing under the weight of junk mail, create thousands of low-skilled jobs, and reduce teen-age unemployment. It would also lead to innovative delivery systems as entrepreneurs strive to cut costs and boost efficiency.[63]

The Postal Board of Governors could unilaterally make this change by a vote at a board meeting. If the governors would not do it, the Justice Department could announce a ruling that the Postal Service's statutory monopoly applies only to first class letters. If the Justice Department would not make this move, a group of third class mailers could bring a test suit against the Postal Service, challenging its interpretation of its monopoly. This approach would put the Postal Service on the defensive, forcing it to publicly insist that it must be allowed to restrain the delivery of numerous diverse items to provide increasingly worse service on first class letters.

Deregulating delivery of junk mail would greatly expand the network of private mail deliverers that, once organized, could create political pressure to abolish the Postal Service's monopoly on first class mail. With a successful private third class delivery system in place, the Postal Service could no longer rely on its usual defense that it must have a monopoly because it is inconceivable that private services would carry letters to all those different houses.

Concurrently, the Postal Service should remove restrictions on the private use of private mailboxes. The Justice Department could also issue a ruling on this, or it could be challenged in court as an uncompensated taking under the Fifth Amendment. Some private delivery services in rural areas have already given their clients free mailboxes, and this is an alternative solution.

The best way to end the postal monopoly is not by launching a debate in which over half a million union members and campaign

---

[63]This proposal is developed from an earlier proposal the author prepared for the Competitive Enterprise Institute, Washington.

contributors fight to the death to remain overpaid and under-worked, but by poking holes in the monopoly and watching competitive services develop. Only after the superiority of private delivery service is demonstrated will there by the momentum to end the monopoly.

The goal should not be to privatize the Post Office, but to end the monopoly and let the Postal Service fend for itself. Once the monopoly is abolished, the Postal Service's revenues will collapse, and then it will be forced to react after public demonstration of its incompetence. The more competition exists, the more incompetent the Postal Service will look, and the less public sympathy will be accorded postal workers.

Privatizing the Postal Service while retaining the postal monopoly would be a pointless charade. This is basically what President Nixon promised in 1970—that the new Postal Service would be efficient, be run like a business, and be free of political patronage. Obviously, this has not happened; the reins of the Postal Service have simply been transferred from Congress to the postal unions and postal bureaucracy. And Congress also continues its meddling.

The notion that some privatization advocates have suggested—that with the right bag of goodies, postal workers will willingly surrender both their monopoly and their lifetime, overpaid jobs—is naive. Career government employees are not risk takers. It makes no sense to try to find the right bribes to make the postal unions surrender their goose that lays the golden eggs.

Deregulation would create thousands of jobs. It would be better to have a million people speedily carrying the mail at $7–$10 an hour than to have 800,000 people cluttering up post offices at $20 an hour. Deregulation would create opportunity for many people, and it would greatly expand the labor market for unskilled workers, allowing them to get excellent experience and a start in the job market.

Conclusion

The United States cannot afford to enter the twenty-first century with a communications system little changed since the eighteenth century. For decades, the Postal Service has promised that it is on the verge of innovations that will make mail service faster and more reliable. And for decades, mail service has slowed while one innovation after another has been abandoned.

At what point will the Postal Service lose its moral right to a monopoly? When no one can have mail delivered at home? When all the mail, not just 40 percent or 50 percent of it, takes two days or more to cross Washington? When the postal workers are paid three times as much as comparable private workers and waste four hours a day, instead of only an hour and a half? How bad do things have to get before we abandon the status quo? Does the United States really need to rely on a system that is suffering from a permanent work slowdown?

In the areas where the Postal Service faces competition, it is getting clobbered. In the areas where the Postal Service does not face competition, it is clobbering its customers. Maybe there is a lesson here.

The United States should recognize that the words "monopoly" and "public service" will almost always be contradictory. The public is best protected when citizens have the right of free choice. We have a choice of blindly trusting to the generosity of government bureaucrats or of relying on competing entrepreneurs. Is there anyone who would say America would be better off if the government outlawed Federal Express and UPS?

Then why should we continue the Postal Service's monopoly over first class mail, simply because our ancestors also endured a postal monopoly? It should not be a federal crime to deliver the mail faster than the U.S. Postal Service.

3. Free the Mail, Part I

James C. Miller III

Virtually everyone agrees that the Postal Service *ought* to be improved. Aside from the weather, perhaps no other single feature of daily life inspires more complaints than the mail. Those who remember the television comedy "Laugh In" may remember the night that Bea Arthur brought down the house with this coy one liner: "Neither snow, nor rain, nor heat, nor gloom of night stays these couriers from the swift completion of their appointed rounds. . . . There must be some other reason."

Suggest that mail service might be improved by ending the government's monopoly over the delivery of letter mail, and most postal officials react as Oscar Wilde did when a producer suggested changes in one of his plays. Wilde clutched his manuscript in mock terror and exclaimed: "Changes? Impossible! Who am I to tamper with a masterpiece!"

To its friends, at least, the Postal Service is a masterpiece—a marvelous mechanical toy, performing its functions with clockwork regularity and precision. Admittedly, the machinery breaks down every now and then, but it only takes a little tinkering—or a modest increase in the price of a first class stamp—to put things right.

But this argument is wearing thin. Criticism of the Postal Service is growing, and its apologists have had to find better excuses. Well, they've tried, but I don't think they've succeeded. Right now, I dare say that among academic researchers there is a nearly unanimous opinion that the private express statutes, which give the U.S. Postal Service a monopoly on letter mail, should be abolished, and sentiments to this effect have been published in both the *New Republic* and the *National Review*.

The author, director of the Office of Management and Budget from 1985 to 1988, is chairman of Citizens for a Sound Economy.

The U.S. Postal Situation

Unfortunately, this view is not shared by officials of the U.S. Postal Service—as distinct from officials of the Reagan and Bush administrations. For if, as it is said, there is nothing quite so compelling as the power of an idea, the major postal interests in the United States seem determined to hold out until the very last. This view is shortsighted, not only from the viewpoint of the users of postal services but also from that of the postal interests themselves.

First, let me describe briefly the organization of postal service in the United States. The U.S. Constitution authorizes, but does not mandate, a government postal service. Until the late 1800s private carriers operated in competition with the U.S. Post Office. The passage of the "private express statutes," however, gave the Post Office exclusive right to carry "letter mail," and over time the power to define such mail has been left to the postal authorities.

In 1970 the U.S. Post Office became the U.S. Postal Service, a corporation ostensibly independent of the federal government but in fact dependent upon it for financial support and maintenance of its monopoly status. It is governed by a board of directors appointed by the president for fixed terms and approved by the Senate. The board appoints the postmaster general, who carries out the board's policies. To limit the discretion of the Postal Service, a five-member Postal Rate Commission reviews, modifies, and approves postal rate increases and major changes in the configuration of services. Although the commission's decisions can be overturned by a unanimous vote of the Postal Service's board of directors, this is seldom done, in part because the commission is wary of reaction from Congress.

The Reagan and Bush administrations, as well as the Postal Rate Commission, have favored long-term reforms in postal services. But such changes have been opposed by Congress, the Postal Service's board, the corporation's management, and, especially, the postal unions.

What are these reforms? Basically, there are three. The first calls for substantial reduction in the taxpayer subsidy that underwrites postal operations. Billions of dollars are spent annually on support of postal employees' pension plans, subsidies for certain classes of mail, and access to financial capital at reduced rates. The second calls for repeal of the private express statutes to allow competition in the delivery of letter mail. And the third calls for eventual privatization of the Postal Service itself.

Why is there such opposition to these reforms? In short, the overwhelming membership of Congress opposes these reforms because of pressure from the unions. The Postal Service is one of the largest employers in the nation, with more than three quarters of a million employees. Every congressional district in every state has thousands of Postal Service employees, many of whom tend to vote solely on whether the candidate supports the Postal Service's position. Members of Congress, therefore, are loath to favor postal reforms that could jeopardize a considerable bloc of votes. And, were this not enough, the postal unions yearly contribute hundreds of thousands of dollars to congressional candidates, most of whom are quite grateful for their support.

The board of the U.S. Postal Service usually opposes these reforms for several reasons. First, given the complexity of the issues and lacking an independent staff of their own, board members tend to become captured by the Postal Service's management. Second, because the administration typically views these appointments as not particularly important in the overall scheme of things, it often chooses people of good character but nonetheless lacking in the zeal necessary to carry out a reform agenda. And third, even if it were inclined to do so, any administration would find it difficult to obtain Senate confirmation of a candidate who professed a commitment to the reforms described above.

The professional management corps of the U.S. Postal Service tends to oppose reform for two reasons. First, like many government employees, they tend to be risk-averse. That is, they know well the current system, operate within its strictures quite nicely, and have little stomach for the uncertainty such reforms would bring. Second, they see little to gain from giving up the Postal Service's monopoly status and having to answer to stockholders instead of appointed officials.

The postal unions oppose reform because they are convinced they have much to lose and little to gain. Certainly, competition would put downward pressure on postal wages. Since enactment of the milestone legislation separating the Post Office from the rest of government, postal wages have risen much faster than wages in either the public or private sector. For most jobs, there are long queues of qualified applicants. Most academic studies of postal wages conclude that postal employees earn a substantial premium that would be eroded if the organization had to compete with the private sector.

Despite this opposition, I believe there will be reform in the U.S. Postal Service—of evolutionary, if not revolutionary, character. The reason is not only the power of the intellectual revolution discussed above but also the existence of widespread discontent with the U.S. Postal Service.

The Postal Service in fact committed a major public relations blunder in December 1987 in its reaction to a congressionally ordered cut in its spending total of less than 1 percent. Rather than trim its staff—indeed, simply forgoing the planned expansion of its Washington headquarters would have sufficed—it shortened window hours by 10 percent, and eliminated the collection and sorting of outgoing mail on Sundays. The Postal Service could have avoided such draconian measures by adopting the recommendations of the General Accounting Office, the Grace Commission, the Privatization Commission, numerous academic studies, and the U.S. Postal Service itself. For example, the Postal Service could have contracted with more retail stores for the sale of stamps, posting of parcel post, and acceptance of express mail. It could also have contracted out larger volumes of mail to private firms for presorting. (Nearly half of all first class mail is sorted by private industry, not by the Postal Service.) Or it could have expanded the practice of contracting out rural mail delivery to private carriers. Fortunately, common sense prevailed (or was it congressional pressure?), and within due time the Postal Service found the needed "savings" in ways that did not inconvenience postal patrons so dramatically.

The real object of this rebellion against the budget cuts was nothing less than elimination of effective congressional oversight and exemption from budgetary discipline. In plain terms, the Postal Service wants to be placed "off budget," exempt from the federal government's need to reduce the federal deficit. I agree that the Postal Service should be placed off budget, but the way to do it is to make the service part of the private sector.

The Postal Service has been an independent government corporation for nearly 20 years. There is no good reason why it should remain part of the federal government, and no good reason why it should enjoy a monopoly over the delivery of letter mail—any more than a single company should enjoy a monopoly over such services as banking, insurance, lawyering, or telecommunications.

But the Postal Service and its unions want it both ways. They want to be an independent corporation when it comes to the budget process, exempt from the belt-tightening and accountability for efficiency required of every other federal agency. At the same time, they want to be a government-protected monopoly when it comes to letter mail, and they want to be a federal agency when it comes to federal subsidies and other benefits. They want to retain the taxpayer payment for revenue forgone, subsidies for the unfunded portion of federal retirement and health benefits, and access to the Federal Financing Bank. As my Daddy used to tell me when I was an argumentative teenager: "Jimmy, you want all the advantages of growing up but none of the responsibilities!"

"What's wrong with competition in this area?" one might ask. After all, isn't competition a national goal articulated by the antitrust laws? The most common argument against competition is the classic monopolist's defense: necessity. If there were no postal monopoly, say the postal monopolists, nationwide delivery of the mail would be left to the caprices and uncertainties of the free market. Mail service no longer would be reliable. Amateurs and fly-by-night operators would move in. The business community would be hampered in its ability to transact business by letter. The economy would suffer. People would be laid off. Calamities untold and manifold would befall the Republic!

As an economist, I am skeptical of these arguments. Have the monopolists never heard of United Parcel Service or Federal Express? If you push them on this point, they will usually come back with the familiar "cream skimming" argument. Yes, they will say, United Parcel and Federal Express are all very well—in their place. But the delivery of letter mail, they argue, is a special situation. If private carriers were permitted to compete for the delivery of letters, competition would be intense for the most profitable routes in highly populated areas, but thinly populated rural areas would be slighted or ignored. Because the Postal Service would be squeezed out of the more profitable routes, it would not be able to take care of the hinterlands. Great-Aunt Gertrude, who lives way up in Lonesome Valley, Montana, would no longer receive cards on Christmas and her birthday.

This argument is likewise unpersuasive. Historically, it has been the private sector that has taken the lead in providing cheaper, faster, and more convenient mail delivery. And it has been the Postal Service that, more often than not, has impeded those efforts by invoking its legal monopoly.

If the Postal Service is really worried about Great-Aunt Gertrude and the other patrons who live on what are supposedly unprofitable routes, why won't it allow competition in those markets, as the Privatization Commission recommends? Why won't it allow competition in the delivery of "junk mail," another recommendation of the commission? Is it afraid of the energy and creativity of the private sector? Does the Postal Service have so little faith in its own employees? Do the postal unions have so little faith in their own members that they think postal workers won't be able to hold their own in competition with private mail carriers?

Well, I don't believe it. As a matter of fact, the 800,000 employees of the U.S. Postal Service are good people. They work hard, raise families, and pay taxes—just like you and me. My problem is not with them—it's with the system, one that is not working particularly well right now. Given an opportunity to compete, I'm sure the Postal Service, including its employees, would do very well indeed.

But simply to repeal the private express statutes and allow private companies to compete would be unfair to the Postal Service as well as inefficient from an economic standpoint. Specifically, as long as the Postal Service remains a governmental entity, it cannot adjust its rates without lengthy administrative hearings; it cannot restructure its operations or introduce other economies without risking the wrath of Congress; and it cannot tie pay to performance and make needed staffing changes because of the political clout of the postal unions. I would make the Postal Service free to compete by cutting completely the umbilical cord to the federal government.

Just over a year ago, I visited several political leaders and privatization experts in Europe. I learned that their public-sector commercial operations have done very well when transferred to the private sector. They have succeeded in part because they have given employees a stake in the outcome. Each employee received shares of stock and incentives to purchase more. Although the employee unions opposed the idea vehemently, their members overwhelmingly took advantage of the stock ownership plan.

As director of the Office of Management and Budget, I put the Reagan administration on record as favoring a privatization approach that would turn over a major portion of the enterprise to Postal Service employees. I favor such an approach for three reasons. First, giving postal employees some compensation for the losses they may incur in having to compete in the marketplace would be equitable. Second, such a move would obviously reduce the opposition of this powerful force. (Turning the Postal Service over to the employees would give each a windfall of *at least* $30,000).

Finally, I believe an employee-owned Postal Service would be a far more efficient operation than the one we witness today. The key is incentives. Give good people the proper incentives and they will work magic. When employees have "a piece of the action," their performance is much better than when they are simply wage earners or salaried employees. Rep. Dana Rohrabacher tells the story of the man who went into a department store around Christmas time—one where the employees have a piece of the action—and found it very crowded. "How are things going?" he asked. "This is the greatest day we ever had!" was the answer. Then he walked across the street to an office of the U.S. Postal Service, and, noticing similar crowds, he asked, "How are things going?" "The worst day we ever had!" came the response. Privatizing the Postal Service and giving postal employees a substantial portion of the ownership would change all that.

As Frank Chodorov observed some 40 years ago in his essay "The Myth of the Post Office," people do not write letters because there is a Postal Service. Rather, the Postal Service exists because people write letters. With the information revolution upon us, surely there's enough business out there for everyone.

One of the most curious, as well as dispiriting, aspects of this issue is that public policy regarding the Postal Service has been at a stalemate for more than a century and a half. The arguments being made today on behalf of the postal monopoly are the very same ones that were made when the private express statutes were enacted. Nor is there much new about the arguments for competition.

However, if the experience of the last 150 years proves anything, it is that the privatizers and antimonopolists have won the argument. Nearly all the great innovations in mail delivery have come from the private sector, while the Postal Service has, at best, tried to catch up or, at worst, tried to stand in the way. The public has everything to gain from competition and little, if anything, to lose. In fact, the only real losers I can imagine would be the cartoonists—who would no longer be able to get belly laughs by depicting the Postal Service as a giant snail.

Victor Hugo once said that nothing can withstand an idea whose time has come. I say it's time to free the mail.

4. Free the Mail, Part II

Daniel Oliver

When the topic turns to the Postal Service, it's tempting merely to recount post office jokes. As postal rates have increased, service has declined, although how one tells it has declined, I don't know. Madison Avenue's new advertising campaign slogan for the Postal Service is, "Remember, you pay more, but you get less." Last week I saw a bumper sticker that I thought was apposite to this topic. It said, "Crime wouldn't pay if the government ran it." If you think it's criminal that the Postal Service has proposed increasing the first class stamp for letters to 32 cents and you're wondering what the extra pennies will pay for, I've discovered the answer: storage.

Joke telling is underrated in our society. Jokes are one way that society expresses its sentiments—often negative. We deride people or institutions in jokes in order to remind ourselves that the butt of the joke deserves it. And so, of course, it is and should be with the Postal Service.

At the same time, however, we have to remember that the Postal Service is not entirely a laughing matter. After all, the Postal Service consumes resources and deprives people of their freedom. That is serious business. And that business, and what might be done about it, is the topic of this paper.

My first point is this: We need not prove here that the Postal Service is inefficient and does not serve consumers well. The evidence, as I understand it, is overwhelming. A New York magazine recently conducted a test which showed that the Postal Service's own claims for speedy delivery were false—though I think not deceptive. How could the claims be false but not deceptive? Well, the claims wouldn't be deceptive unless people believed them.

And that, of course, is part of the problem. Many people know the Postal Service is second rate. I have received more mail in

The author was chairman of the Federal Trade Commission from 1985 to 1989.

response to my comments about the Postal Service than about any other single issue. A serviceman in Europe wrote to complain about the slowness and inaccuracy of mail delivery. He actually wrote twice, the second time to ask how he could support privatization. But some people still put trust in government and believe what politicians tell them, even though the warning on our coins is plain: "In God We Trust." Some people will believe the politicians who tell them that postal service is good and is improving. But then some people believe that President Reagan's tax cuts caused the budget deficit.

Some wag recently described the Postal Service as "one of the most efficient . . . operations in the world." You and I know that's nonsense. After all, how would we tell if it's efficient? What would we compare it with? People thought manual typewriters were efficient too—until electric typewriters came along—and they were in turn replaced by word processors. What we do know about the Postal Service is that in areas where it does compete—in the overnight mail delivery business—it's a failure. We may reasonably conclude that the rest of the operation is a failure too.

Indeed, simply because the Postal Service is a monopoly, we can and must assume it does not serve consumers well. We are entitled to make that assumption by virtue of the existence, history, and modern mainstream interpretations of the Sherman Act, the Clayton Act, and the Federal Trade Commission Act. These are essentially antimonopoly statutes or, perhaps more accurately, anticartel statutes. It's also true, of course, that there are "natural monopolies," but we need not be concerned with that issue either because clearly the Postal Service is not a natural monopoly. A natural monopoly doesn't need the full panoply of congressional protection and posturing to protect it. The antimonopoly, anticartel statutes are embodiments of our society's determination that monopolies are detrimental to our economic health and to consumers. Those who seriously assert either that the Postal Service is efficient or can be made to work well are really raising far more fundamental questions about our antitrust statutes. And they should be made to answer those questions. In short, because the Postal Service is a monopoly, we know, a priori, that consumers lose out when they deal with it.

My second point can be stated as a question: Given that the Postal Service is inefficient and disserves consumers, is there nevertheless some reason for keeping it in its present form? Does it perform a special function or serve a purpose that justifies its preservation as a monopoly in a society that opposes monopolies?

The answer is no. Some people will say the answer is yes, but they are wrong. They say that without the government-protected Postal Service, people who live off the beaten track will be denied mail service or will have to pay exorbitant prices for it. This is essentially the argument that mail service is so important that its preservation and operation must be guaranteed and supervised by government.

But how important is mail service? Is mail as important as medicine? Is mail as important as food? As important as clothing? Medicine, food, and clothing are delivered throughout this land by private enterprises. If those essential goods can reach northern North Dakota, southern New Mexico, and the wilderness of Appalachia, then, surely, so can the mail. Newspapers reach rural areas through private efforts. So can the mail—if necessary, by piggybacking onto the services that deliver the other goods people in rural areas depend on. Clearly, then, there is no justification for the monopoly status of the Postal Service.

My third point is also in the nature of a question: What should be done with the Postal Service? There are several options. Some people say it should be privatized—sold off to private interests— and that's fine with me. What is most important, however, is that the Postal Service be demonopolized. If the government wants to continue to own it and try to compete with private enterprises— well, good luck. But there can be no subsidies. Taxpayers should not be forced to subsidize an inefficient organization when there are efficient ones ready to perform the job. The sight of government trying to compete with private enterprise would provide a useful lesson for those who remain, still, unaware of the limitations of the state.

More realistically, perhaps, a single class of service—for example, addressed third class mail—could be demonopolized, that is, exempted from the private express statutes that grant a monopoly to the Postal Service. That is essentially what happened with overnight mail. Business went to the Postal Service and to Congress and said, "Look, we can't do business this way. There has to be an exemption for allowing private enterprise to provide reliable, overnight delivery, across town or across the country." And so Federal Express was born along with its imitators and competitors, which include in name but not in fact the Postal Service's own loosely named "Express Mail." But Express Mail, of course, is anything but a success, and consumers know it. The Postal Service's share of the overnight letter business has reportedly fallen 60 percent in the last year.

As a practical, political matter, it may be possible to obtain another exemption for a single class of mail, and we should at least consider settling for that much in the short run. Such a settlement, however, should not be viewed as capitulation to a postal monopoly.

My fourth and final point is addressed to the new Postmaster General Anthony Frank.

Washington is a political town. Regardless of why you came here, you will have to be, or become, competent at politics if you are to be successful.

But what does "successful" mean? Perhaps I should ask, "what should it mean?" In my judgment, being successful means serving the general interest of the nation as a whole—I call it the consumer interest, because it is only as consumers, not as producers, that we have many common interests. Being successful means serving the general interest, not a special interest.

The sad truth is that the Postal Service is a special interest. And, Mr. Frank, you must decide whether you are here to serve that special interest or to serve the general interest, namely, the interest of American consumers of mail delivery service. You cannot serve both interests. They are antithetical.

Your predecessor, Preston Tisch, also had a terrific reputation as a businessman. But I think it is fair to say that his tenure as postmaster general was not successful. He will be remembered, if he is remembered at all, as the man responsible for the rate increase to 25 cents and for Saturday closings. How those two measures serve consumers is not instantly apparent.

What was Tisch's mistake? He treated the Postal Service's problems as a management problem. Mr. Frank, you have also said that you are "dedicated to increasing efficiency." But that is the businessman's approach—that was Preston Tisch's approach—and I think the wrong approach.

As I've pointed out, the Postal Service is a monopoly, and monopolies behave like monopolies no matter who's in charge of them. To say you are going to make the monopolistic Postal Service efficient is like saying that you have decided to weigh 40 pounds less tomorrow. In one case you plan to defy the laws of economics; in the other you plan to defy the law of gravity. You can claim that you don't believe in the law of gravity, but that's different from defying it. Apples fall in a downward direction and strike heads, both the heads of people who haven't even discovered the law of gravity yet and the heads of those who plan to exempt themselves from it. You can no more defy the laws of economics than you can defy the law of gravity. Even you, Mr. Frank, cannot make an unnatural monopoly serve the American consumers efficiently.

You may be able to make some ever so marginal improvements by tinkering with knobs and dials. But I urge you to consider whether there isn't a better way to serve the American people. Did you come all the way from California to tinker?

I think there is a better way to serve the American people. But the way I recommend is managing the politics, not the economics, of the Postal Service.

And make no mistake: Politics is what it's all about. The Postal Service employs some 800,000 workers, making it the third largest organization in the world after the Chinese and Soviet armies. That's 800,000 constituents/voters, whose average wage is estimated to be about 25 percent higher than comparable wages in the private sector. A Letter Carrier Union chief said recently, "We made out like bandits in our new contracts." The excess portion of those wages—the part that's higher than what competition would allow—is what economists call "monopoly rents." A portion of those monopoly rents is always available for lobbying to preserve those rents for Postal Service employees. That's the way politics works.

Following is an example of politics at work. A few years ago I made some comments about the Postal Service similar to those I have made here. Not long afterward, a gentleman who works on Capitol Hill asked the General Accounting Office to investigate whether the sums the FTC had spent on materials discussing the postal monopoly were "necessary, appropriate, consistent with the Commission's mission and in accord with law." The intent of initiating that investigation, I suspect, was to fire a warning shot across my bow: Leave the 800,000 alone.

So, having said all that, what do I recommend that the postmaster general do? You must manage the politics. You must understand that serving the American people in this case requires a political solution to their problem. You must stand up and in a loud voice call for an end to the monopoly status of the Postal Service.

Will Congress respond? Not right away, of course—except perhaps to investigate how much time you spent talking to me. Nevertheless, you'll be planting the seed of an idea which will not flower overnight. Such things take time in Washington: It is not a business community. Consider how long it took, for example, to reduce the income tax rates: They said it couldn't be done, and then Ronald Reagan came along. These things take time, and they take leadership. And leadership is what you have to provide. A call by the Postmaster General for demonopolization of the Postal Service will be heard more clearly than a call by any other person, save perhaps the president.

Such a stance will not make you popular. Those 800,000 postal employees have friends in high places. You won't be wined and dined in Georgetown, or sit in the posh boxes at the Kennedy Center. But you didn't come here from California for that, did you? The food, and certainly the wine, is better in California, as, surely, is the entertainment. But unless you decide to stand up and be a genuine American hero, your fate will be much like that of your predecessor: forgotten. I do not suggest it will be easy. You will have to excel at politics and theater, and be as brave and as resolute as John Wayne and Charlton Heston, who after all faced only angry mobs and hordes.

Mr. Frank, don't let the political elements keep you from your appointed round. You have a chance to make a profound difference, one that may not come your way again.

I want to conclude by quoting from a letter I sent to your predecessor—Mr. . . . What's-his-name, you know, the fellow who gave us the 25 cent stamp and Saturday closings:

> If we as a nation really believe in competition, we should advocate it for mail service as we do for other industries. If the idea proves to be unpopular, then we must ask ourselves, "Do we really believe in competition?" Or is all our

talk about "competitiveness" and antitrust enforcement just so much lip-service we pay to the idea of competition—all the while pursuing anti-competitive exemptions for special interests?

Bear in mind, the mail monopoly is not just an idle anachronism. It is a government statute that prevents our citizens from employing mail carriers of their choice. It interferes with their liberty—in this case their liberty to contract for efficient mail delivery service. The point of repealing the monopoly is not to obtain better delivery service for letters. Letters don't have rights. People do. The point of repealing the monopoly statute is to increase the liberty of our citizens.

By calling for an end to the postal monopoly, you have a chance to become a genuine hero to consumers and to all who believe in free markets and competition. You have a noble opportunity to serve the cause of liberty. . . .

Mr. Frank, I wish you all the best.

5. Efficiency, Yes; Balkanization, No

Anthony M. Frank

My mother used to tell me everything is achievable in this world except maintaining the status quo. You can go backward or forward, but you cannot stay the same. I've built my career on anticipating and managing change, and I expect to continue doing just that during my tenure in the Postal Service.

In California my wife and I have always enjoyed the outdoors, particularly rock climbing. When a rock climber ascends a rock face, he tests out every new handhold before he lets go of the old one. In the Postal Service, as we approach an uncharted and rapidly changing future, we must also test and probe to ensure we are always moving forward securely and responsibly.

What I would like to do here is examine what is meant by the term "privatization," because, frankly, despite all the headlines and heat, I sense some hesitancy, even among the most ardent privatizers. I sense a desire to go slowly and a recognition that the mail system, like Humpty Dumpty, once broken, couldn't be put back together again.

So what does privatization mean? Does it mean throwing out the private express statutes, thereby eliminating the letter-mail monopoly? If so, I am against it, because I believe the U.S. Postal Service is a legitimate and necessary *public* institution that serves an important social function as a binding, unifying force in our national life. Government should continue to provide mail service on a fair and equitable basis to all citizens.

Is privatization simply a code word for union busting? If it is, I'm not in the business of union busting, and I do not intend to reopen any contract negotiations.

Is privatization an attempt to let private companies selectively skim off the profitable segments of postal business and leave the

The author is postmaster general of the United States.

Postal Service to serve those groups and areas deemed unprofitable? If it is, I oppose it because I believe we must preserve the economic base that supports our ability to provide universal service at uniform, affordable rates.

Is privatization, on the other hand, a genuine effort to promote efficiency in the Postal Service by increasing work-sharing initiatives with major mailers and contracting with the private sector for more noncritical postal services? If so, I am certainly interested in exploring what more can be done in these areas.

I am from the private sector and know well the virtues of competition. I have no automatic negative reaction to proposals for more private-sector involvement in the mail business. But neither do I accept the broad-brush picture painted by critics who claim that nothing in the Postal Service works.

In fact, the U.S. Postal Service is working pretty well. It can work better, and I guarantee that changes are coming. But, on balance, it is a remarkably efficient operation, given its size and the breadth of services it provides. The following numbers illustrate my point:

- The U.S. Postal Service handles more than 500 million pieces of mail every business day. That's more than twice the volume handled by Federal Express in a year, and the Postal Service handles more pieces in one week than United Parcel Service does in a year.
- The U.S. Postal Service provides daily mail delivery six days a week to more than 95 million addresses across the country. It has added an average of 1.7 million new delivery addresses annually over the last five years.
- The U.S. Postal Service receives no direct federal subsidy for operations. Its appropriation covers the cost of actual services provided at preferred, or free, rates at the express direction of Congress.

As these numbers make clear, no private company today even remotely approaches the size or the experience of the U.S. Postal Service in providing all types of mail service to all locations and every individual address throughout the country. I do not believe the American people want to lose this convenient, affordable public service. I believe they want it to be even more convenient and no less affordable in the future. The real challenge, then, is to improve the efficiency of our operations and constrain costs while continuing to improve service for all customers, large and small.

The fewer times the Postal Service must handle a letter, the more efficient it is said to be. Efficiency is enhanced when mail is presorted to 9-digit ZIP Codes or carrier routes, prepared for processing on such high-speed equipment as our optical character reader/bar-code sorter, and deposited in bulk in a mail processing center. Such "efficient" mail is typically generated by a business mailer.

Obviously, not all mail can be so "efficient." All of us individually hand address letters and cards, which may or may not include a correct 5-digit ZIP Code, and deposit these along with our bills, a few at a time, in the neighborhood mailbox. Such mail is much less "efficient" than the business mailer's but no less deserving of service.

The point I am making is not simplistic, and it goes to the heart of much of the debate about efficiency in the Postal Service. As a public institution, it serves *all* the American people, not merely those groups, areas, or segments that are clearly profitable.

We can and do, of course, encourage efficiency through incentive discounts to major mailers for certain types of work sharing. We will continue to support and expand work-sharing efforts that make good economic sense for both business mailers and the Postal Service. But we will also continue to provide *universal* mail service at uniform rates to every American, and to give attention to the quality of service for individuals as well as large, profitable mailers.

Efficiency is a factor not only of day-to-day operations but also of management's overall ability to control and apply its resources in response to the marketplace. I find it particularly ironic that those who complain the loudest about Postal Service inefficiency and the need for competition are the very same ones who took the lead within the Reagan administration in *tying our hands* in the 1987 Omnibus Budget Reconciliation Act. According to them, a dollar spent for capital investment is no different from a dollar spent on paper clips. They sought to limit the discretion of the Postal Service to use its resources as it judged best. What private business could operate efficiently under such outside intrusion?

I am deeply concerned about the long-term implications of the wrenching cuts imposed on the Postal Service's capital improvement programs in December 1987, and even more concerned that the mailing public not be required to underwrite further deficit reduction efforts in the future. If we want greater efficiency in the Postal Service—and believe me, I do—we must not tie management's hands. Management must have discretion to apply postal resources in the best interest of postal business, and it must have pricing flexibility to respond to market competition.

All of us in the Postal Service are acutely aware of the ongoing need for serious and permanent measures to control costs and improve productivity. We manage a very large system that can and must be improved in significant ways. We also recognize that a healthy Postal Service must avoid simply passing along every cost increase through higher rates.

Perhaps the most obvious answer to the problems of efficiency and cost containment is technology. For example, first class, letter-size mail can be sorted manually at a rate of 800 pieces per work hour. Mechanical sortation processes 1,850 pieces per work hour, and fully automated technology handles 10,000 pieces per work hour.

In 1983 the Postal Service initiated deployment of a full-scale automation program scheduled for completion in 1989. The total cost of this program is approximately $750 million. As a result, labor requirements in 1987 were 23,000 work years below what they otherwise would have been. That translates into a savings of $750 million in labor costs. Additional efficiencies are being gained through work-sharing programs in which business mailers perform a good deal of the work before they deposit their mail. In return, they pay discounted rates.

We are in the process of creating a group of Postal Service and industry representatives to identify additional opportunities for work sharing. We are now developing guidelines for the group, which will seek tangible ideas for substantial new work-sharing efforts that would reduce costs for both mailers and the Postal Service. More work sharing and more automation are two essential ways to improve efficiency and hold down costs. Other potential areas for improved efficiency and savings—for example, curbside and cluster-box delivery systems in newly developed areas—require a degree of public acceptance that hasn't been fully gained yet, and I'm not certain it ever will be. Canada, for example, has recently tried the cluster-box approach, or "super mail boxes." The initiative has been roundly criticized by both large and small postal customers.

The Postal Service must also do more contracting out in situations where it will achieve real cost savings. Contracted services now account for roughly 10 percent of annual Postal Service expenditures.

The Postal Service already contracts with private companies for virtually all mail transportation beyond the local area. It is also pursuing efforts to sell stamps at no more than face value through major grocery chains and other retail outlets. This not only expands the retail network at minimal cost but, equally important, also makes an essential postal service much more accessible and convenient for most people.

Contracting out is no different from the "make or buy" decisions made every day by businesses throughout the country. We already make these decisions, and we intend to do more of this when it makes sense.

Automation, work sharing, and contracted services are areas we will continue to address as part of the Postal Service's commitment to improve the efficiency of its operations and the quality of its service. This is certainly my personal commitment as postmaster general. But, to return to the analogy of the rock climber, we must test and probe thoroughly as we proceed. We want to avoid the problems other countries have experienced in their attempts to make their postal systems more profitable.

In Great Britain, for example, a Christian bookseller paid approximately $88,500 for the right to have the country use "Jesus Is Alive" as its cancellation stamp through the Easter holiday. This is hardly the kind of private enterprise most Americans would find compatible with a constitutional commitment to the separation of church and state. In a similar but more serious vein, on April 1, 1987, New Zealand restructured its postal-telecommunications-banking system into separate government enterprises, each with a mandate to be profitable. As a result, the postal enterprise determined to close one-third of its 1,200 post offices as uneconomical, a policy it is aggressively implementing. Again, I suspect this approach would not be popular with the American people.

We want to avoid mistakes and missteps. We want our progress to be sure and lasting. But above all, we want progress—and we will have it in the Postal Service.

I have not espoused the traditional arguments of those who support our present postal system. These include questions about

51

how, in a balkanized private system, the sanctity and security of the mails could be ensured, how it would deal with labor strikes and bankruptcies, and where change-of-address notices would be sent. Neither have I touched on the complexities of managing international mail in a world postal system of 168 sovereign nations that cooperate to ensure the secure flow of mail and proper exchange of postal payments within the world community.

These are all important considerations. These and many other practical issues would have to be addressed in any comprehensive debate on the merits of privatization. In not raising them specifically, I do not mean in any way to minimize their importance.

But my purpose here has been to attempt to focus on precisely what is meant by the term "privatization." Is it immediate, total postal entrepreneurism? Is it a thinly disguised attempt to destroy the postal unions? Is it a move to let private companies skim the profitable segments of the business? Or is it an effort to encourage more work sharing and contracting out in the name of efficiency?

I believe the U.S. Postal Service is a necessary and proper public institution. Together, its employees and management can adapt and change to better serve the changing needs of the American people. I see my job as helping the Postal Service to anticipate change and respond in ways that promote the common good.

To do this, the Postal Service must have greater discretion to manage its finances and plan and invest to meet future needs efficiently. It must also have greater flexibility in setting rates in order to respond to competitors and provide work-sharing incentives where these represent real cost improvement to both the mailer and the Postal Service.

I may be naive, but why must the arguments always be "either or"? Are we positive there is no middle ground? In my view the Postal Service should *not* be a for-profit institution. It should be the most efficient, reliable, convenient public service in the country.

In fact, the Postal Service is a much more efficient, productive business enterprise than its critics acknowledge. Contrary to popular wisdom in some quarters, productivity increases since reorganization are comparable to those in the nonfarm private-sector economy. Although postal employees received substantial wage increases in the early 1970s, over the last decade employee wage increases have tracked with inflation and have generally corresponded to wage increases in the nonfarm private sector. The Postal

Service is not deficit ridden; indeed, over the decade it has produced a slight surplus of $560 million, or 0.2 percent above the break-even point for the period. There's a great deal more information that clearly refutes assertions about inefficiency and ineptitude in the Postal Service.

To conclude, then, the Postal Service is an old and established public institution that is a vital link in the economic and social life of the United States. Like most large enterprises today, private or public, it is experiencing change and competition. Our commitment is to manage that change constructively and to make the Postal Service a better public service—in terms of cost and quality—that is provided fairly and equitably to all the American people.

6. Privatization, Yes

John Crutcher

Five years ago I made my first proposal on privatizing the Postal Service in a speech at Harvard University. I advocated a wide range of experimentation in contracting out postal retail, mail processing, and delivery functions. That speech brought down a minor firestorm of protest. The League of Postmasters hired a law firm to threaten legal action, postal officials protested angrily, and some press comments were less than laudatory.

At the time I thought, naively as it turned out, that I would have active and public support from large mailers and their organizations. Nearly all of them patted me on the back privately and said they liked my ideas, but none of them gave vigorous public backing and support. Now after five frustrating years, I rejoice that a large segment of the mailing industry is publicly advocating more contracting out as one way to reduce postal costs. It has come a long way in five years.

Recently, the Third Class Mail Association made it known, vigorously and publicly, that contracting out various parts of the postal operation, a form of privatization, has the potential to save enormous sums of money and consequently result in fewer rate increases. Lee Epstein, speaking for the association, gave some pointed advice to the postmaster general:

> Don't go to the negotiating table unless you're resolved to walk away with the least costly of any previous contracts, . . . satisfying yourself with anything less just won't do. Don't be willing to walk away from the table without getting the work rule changes to provide the work force flexibility necessary to provide postal services as cost efficiently as possible. Don't go to the negotiating table without knowing well in advance the benefits that can be derived from contracting work out to the private sector rather than keeping

The author is a commissioner on the Postal Rate Commission.

all tasks in-house. And don't look on contracting out merely as a negotiating ploy, . . . if contracting out can produce real savings then do it. Don't come to the rate commission with a request for new rates without also coming with new work-sharing, postal rate discount programs in hand. Mailers are tired and disgusted with seeing the Postal Service dismiss and oppose mailer-sponsored work-sharing proposals, and expecting us to bear quietly the cost burdens caused by inefficiencies and excesses.

All segments of the postal industry and much of the public are upset about the very large increases in postal costs. Such increases are soon translated into increased rates. Some anger has been directed at the rate commission for not trimming postal cost increases in its recent rate decision. The commission members looked very hard at the increases and frankly were also appalled. Unfortunately, the commission's enabling legislation prescribes that rates be sufficient to allow the service to break even, so that is what the commission attempted to do. The courts have severely limited the Postal Rate Commission's ability to disallow Postal Service costs.

Many mailers have said, "Postal costs are out of control." I believe that a modest step would be for mailers and their respective associations from all four classes to band together to document and publicize informed criticism of postal cost increases and recommend appropriate management reforms. This might take the form of a newly created mailers' group to monitor USPS management and issue a quarterly or semiannual report assessing its performance regarding cost control. These reports would be quoted in the press, in Congress, and throughout the bureaucracy. If they are skillfully prepared, postal management would have to respond. Such reports could motivate management to be more responsive, more creative, and certainly more cooperative. This new "watchdog" would represent everyone interested in better postal performance, so that no firm or interest group would be seen as its principal sponsor. There is plenty of room for inclusion of public-service representatives like Ralph Nader and the Postal Rate Commission's Office of the Consumer Advocate. Although it is difficult for all the mailers and consumer representatives to agree on postal policy issues, the issue of reducing postal costs is surely one interest they have in common.

Mailers should heed Benjamin Franklin's advice to his fellow signers of the Declaration of Independence, "We must all hang together, or assuredly we shall all hang separately."

I have sometimes compared the U.S. Postal Service with a mighty battleship in the U.S. Navy. The Captain, standing on the bridge, sees danger ahead and shouts orders to the helmsman: "Hard right rudder." The helmsman dutifully swings the wheel sharply right, but the ship plows on in the same direction, seemingly for an eternity, until finally it begins to respond very slowly to the rudder. The USPS is like that battleship, only worse. The postmaster general can give commands to his subordinates but changes in course come very, very slowly.

A host of impediments can block changes in postal policy. During the 1984 labor contract negotiations, for example, the postmaster general had been instructed by the board of governors to hold out for a starting wage lower than the prevailing $21,500 for new employees. When the contract expired, William Bolger, feeling free from that constraint, began hiring new employees at a lower salary. Union and management organizations complained loudly to Congress, which passed a law with astonishing speed to prohibit new hiring except under terms of the old contract. Amazingly, the vote was bipartisan and almost unanimous. The postal unions and management organizations have friends in high places.

The U.S. Postal Service, of course, enjoys a monopoly for the carriage and delivery of all letter mail. But the Postal Service defines the limits of its own monopoly. I have long held that it is unreasonable to arbitrarily exclude the householder's mailbox from delivery by locally based, community oriented, nonprofit organizations for which the federal taxpayer now pays a subsidy of $436 million. If the boy scouts want to earn a few bucks by delivering the weekly bulletins of the local Methodist and Catholic churches, why not tip your hat to them and rejoice that they are saving the federal taxpayer a small sum, relieving local mail carriers of a small portion of their back-breaking burden, ensuring accurate and speedy delivery of the product, and in the process giving the boy scouts an opportunity to learn what work is all about. The Postal Service has disdained this modest suggestion, implying that all sorts of dire consequences might flow from such a radical change in the rules. Such objections boil down to a simple determination to maintain the Postal Service's stranglehold on the mailbox, ignoring the logic of simple relaxation of a rule that in the long run has some potential to benefit taxpayers and the service itself to a modest degree.

A large segment of the private mailing industry, namely, the Third Class Mail Association, has been clamoring for a more radical change in the mailbox rule. Dr. Gene Del Polito, executive director of the association, says that the symbiotic relationship between the Postal Service and the association has deteriorated over the past several years because of poor mail service, rising postal rates, and the prospect for even higher rates in the offing, perhaps as soon as spring 1991. He notes that the mail advertising industry has no power to control Postal Service costs, almost 85 percent of which are labor related. Those businesses, he claims, are caught on the horns of a dilemma—out-of-control postal costs on one hand and the prohibition of competition for the delivery of advertising and other business related mail on the other.

The Third Class Mail Association petitioned the postmaster general to initiate a rule-making proceeding that would lead to suspension of the letter mail monopoly over the carriage of addressed third class mail. It came as no surprise to anyone in the mailing industry that the postmaster general denied the request, but this denial does not mean that the issue will simply die. There is too much evidence at hand to indicate that private carriers can do a cheaper and more reliable job of delivering advertising matter. In several parts of the United States, including some rural areas, private carriers, serving established routes on a regular basis, already deliver advertising mail to householders having alternative private mailboxes. And they do this for less cost than the U.S. Postal Service. Many private delivery routes exactly parallel those of the Postal Service. If the Postal Service were genuinely interested in providing more reliable service at lower cost, it would experiment widely with contracting with those same private carriers to deliver all the mail, including that which they now deliver. Postmaster General Anthony Frank has said quite forcefully that he wants to examine contracting out as one major way to provide better service and save Postal Service dollars.

I am reminded of an old *New Yorker* cartoon showing the Salvation Army band positioned close to a man lying dead drunk in the gutter. The director of the band says, "It looks like this is a good place to start!" There are several good places to start contracting out mail services. The service already contracts with hundreds of independent truckers to private services over what are called "star routes." These are exclusive franchises to carry mail between specific locations on a scheduled basis. Some star routes in rural areas also provide delivery services to businesses and residences. Thus there are existing models within the service for further expansion of the private sector into the delivery function. There are many other areas in which the Postal Service could improve its performance through greater cooperation with the private sector.

The heightened interest in improving the USPS is encouraging. Many distinguished economic scholars, including James Miller III of OMB and Thomas Gale Moore, have recommended abolishing the private express statutes. Others have advanced various schemes to simply sell the USPS to its employees. All of those proposals, although attractive from an economic standpoint, are simply impossible for political reasons. The five major postal unions and postal management organizations are very powerful and evenly dispersed in every congressional district. I don't think you could get 12 of the 435 members of Congress or four senators to put their names on a bill to repeal the private express statutes—and half of those would probably plan to retire before the next election.

Many believe that postal unions are the problem, but in fact postal management is far more at fault. Management actually has a great disincentive to control labor costs. After each major contract is negotiated, management salaries rise by a percentage roughly reflecting bargaining-unit increases, surely a colossal disincentive for tough bargaining. It is difficult to think of another system in which management's rewards are scaled not to savings achieved by tough bargaining but to savings lost.

I have no personal vendetta against postal management. Senior postal officials I have met and worked with are invariably friendly, outgoing people who understand their jobs exceedingly well. They work hard and are dedicated to the service, but they are, with few exceptions, creatures of the bureaucratic system from whence they came. It is a system that devours its young, especially those who are innovative and creative. There is little payoff in the service for those who challenge the establishment with new ideas and disturb their superiors with creative thoughts. By the time managers work their way up through the multilayered bureaucracy to senior positions, they are rarely willing to get out of step with their peers by promoting fundamental changes, no matter how badly they are needed. Career managers are conditioned and molded to go along with convention. Advocating reform did not get them where they are today and might even threaten their preeminence in the system tomorrow. Why rock the boat?

The single best avenue to improve productivity and control costs in the service is contracting out in those areas I have mentioned. This would require no change in the law, and in most cases, no changes even in union labor agreements. The only requirement is determination on the part of postal governors and the postmaster general to implement policy decisions directing management to become more creative in contracting for services. The future health of the USPS depends on this form of privatization.

7. The Federal Postal Monopoly: History, Rationale, and Future

Thomas Gale Moore

The delivery of cards, letters, and packages seems to be one of the most benign of the federal government's activities. Unlike the draft or federal taxation, in the popular imagination, the post office presents a fairly friendly face. To suggest that postal services should be privatized, therefore, has the air of iconoclasm. One might as well attack motherhood or apple pie. This was not always the case, however. The United States has a long tradition of resistance to the postal monopoly of the federal government. The private express statutes in their current form, in fact, date from the last decisive battle in which Post Office supporters reasserted the monopoly power of the government to stamp out spreading private mail service. I will review very briefly the history of the postal monopoly in the United States and discuss the complete or partial repeal of the statutes.[1] The history of the federal postal monopoly reveals how the Post Office has protected its rents over the decades, and provides some lessons we do well to heed.

Like many of the functions of the modern state, the postal power took its first leap forward during wartime. The American revolutionaries needed fast and reliable channels of communication to the army and the state legislatures. The Continental Congress undertook management of the post, there being no other organization that could provide such national service. Fearing loss of postal revenues from competition at a time when every available dollar

The author was a member of the President's Council of Economic Advisers during the Reagan administration.

[1]The best history of the postal monopoly is George Priest, "The History of the Postal Monopoly in the United States," *Journal of Law and Economics* 18, no. 33 (1975). Several criticisms of the postal monopoly made in this paper have been adapted from Priest's article.

61

was needed for the war effort, Congress passed postal monopoly statutes as early as 1782.

By 1787, when the Constitution was framed, the need for a nationalized, war-emergency-style post had disappeared. There can be little doubt, however, that the framers intended to authorize such a congressionally controlled national postal service. Fortunately, while the Constitution authorizes such a national monopoly, it does not require it. We may reasonably suppose that the framers wanted a national postal service, but wanted the government to provide it only so long as it was the only organization capable of doing so.

Whatever the intentions of the framers, however, it did not take long for the federal government, and the Federalist party that initially controlled it, to discover that postal services were a powerful political tool. The government-sponsored post kept the denizens of the frontiers abreast of the services their representatives in Washington were rendering on their behalf, by means of letters from their congressional members and newspapers and magazines. Both the government "frank" and special low rates for newspapers and magazines are features of the federal postal monopoly that have endured to the present day. By 1800, service was provided to the furthest western and southern frontiers. This broad expansion of routes coincided with the transfer of control over establishing postal routes from the president to Congress. Congress dealt with the problem of choosing among postal routes by the simple expedient of expanding routes indiscriminately, financing the expansion by charging monopoly prices on the highly profitable eastern routes.

To maintain these rents, Congress had to revise the monopoly provisions of the postal statutes regularly, plugging the leaks that sprang up as individuals sought more economical means to convey their mail. In 1792, 1827, 1836, and 1838, Congress passed laws to strengthen the monopoly that provided the revenues to finance postal expansion. Even with strenuous efforts to prop up the monopoly, however, the ability and willingness of eastern mailers to subsidize the mail in the South and West was limited. Dissatisfaction with high postage rates grew. In 1843, it cost as much to send a letter from New York City to Troy, New York, as it did a barrel of flour.

Private express firms, which were already well established by the 1820s, came into their own as midcentury approached. Especially in the delivery of time-sensitive mail and negotiable instruments, private expresses flourished, in part because they were more willing to guarantee safe delivery. Presaging today's Express Mail, in 1825 the Post Office set up an express mail service to compete with private messenger services, but it failed and was discontinued in 1839.

By the 1840s private mail services had spread out from the financial markets and the newspaper business and into the delivery of personal mail. Much of this was illegal, of course, but many citizens used the private services anyway. The Post Office first resorted to the courts, suing Commodore Vanderbilt's steamship company for transporting mail in violation of the federal law. The Post Office lost the suit, however, on technical grounds that suggested the postal monopoly statutes were all but unenforceable. The decision made clear that, in the absence of new legal barriers, the business of the Post Office would be taken over, at least on the profitable East Coast routes, entirely by the private express firms.

This was the moment of truth for the federal monopoly Post Office. As you might well surmise, the cause of free enterprise and economic efficiency did not prevail. The private express statutes, which effectively eradicated the private express companies, were the upshot of the political crisis that developed around the issue of postal services in 1844 and 1845. Why did Congress feel compelled to make sure that private competition did not infringe on the federal postal monopoly? The main reason seems to have been the imperative of maintaining contact with the far-flung reaches of the new American empire that was extending itself almost daily across the continent. (The cross-subsidization which Congress forbade in the Postal Reorganization Act of 1970 was the deliberate policy which Congress reaffirmed in the 1840s with the private express statutes.) With its monopoly power, the Post Office could extract rents which could be used in turn to subsidize the frontier postal routes.

The logic of the postal monopoly has remained with us right up to the present day. Financing unprofitable routes through monopoly rents has obvious political benefits that have driven the expansion of the Post Office over the decades. The costs of high rates and deteriorating service have led periodically to groundswells of dissatisfaction with the federal government's postal service, to which the Post Office has responded in various ways.

The most recent wave of dissatisfaction led to the Postal Reorganization Act of 1970. In this law, Congress abolished the Post Office as a cabinet-level department in the executive branch and replaced it with an independent corporation. The new Postal Service was not allowed to operate with the same freedom, however, as a private corporation. It was still required to maintain universal service, even to money-losing locations. Congress did not intend these costly routes to be cross-subsidized by the more profitable urban routes, however. Rather, Congress promised to make up in annual appropriations any loss incurred by the Postal Service in serving the less profitable routes.

With the justification for the federal postal monopoly removed by the promise of congressional appropriation to cover expenditures on money-losing routes, there was no longer any need to maintain the prohibition against private expresses, even if one accepted the rationale that the provision of universal postal service was the duty of the government. Congress, indeed, asked the new Postal Service to review the private express statutes and consider whether they were still needed. Not surprisingly, the Postal Service concluded in its 1973 report that the federal postal monopoly should be continued for the public good. The report's recommendations were basically followed, and the Postal Service continues to exercise a legal monopoly over first class and some kinds of third class mail.

In the report, the governors of the Postal Service made several different arguments for maintaining the private express statutes. Generally speaking, the governors' arguments rested on the theory that postal services are a natural monopoly, and this economic fact justifies the preservation of the private express statutes. This appeal to economic theory is unconvincing at best. As our casual review of the history of the postal monopoly suggests, the Post Office did not evolve as a natural monopoly, gradually increasing its size, taking advantage of economies of scale, and driving out competitors. To the contrary, repeated, vigorous, and ever-expanding efforts by the federal government were necessary to stamp out the private firms that sprang up over the years to meet consumers' demands for faster, more secure, and less expensive delivery service. The notion that a natural monopoly should *require* legal barriers against competitors in order to survive is equally absurd. A natural monopoly will not need legal barriers to maintain its position—hence the term *natural* monopoly. Moreover, there is the additional fact that virtually no evidence suggests postal services enjoy significant economies of scale. One can hardly avoid the conclusion that the natural monopoly argument is nothing more than special pleading for the Postal Service, with a thin veneer of economic theory.

Another argument advanced in the 1973 report is that if private firms could enter the postal services market, they would "skim the cream," competing with the Postal Service in the profitable routes or categories of service, but not in the less profitable ones. This claim, however, is inconsistent with the scheme envisioned by the 1970 act. Unless some customers are paying excessive rates in order to subsidize service to other customers, there should be no cream to skim. In the 1970 act, Congress was attempting to get away from the cross-subsidization that makes cream-skimming possible. Repealing the private express statutes and allowing private firms to compete would result in cream-skimming, therefore, only if there are cross-subsidies to be eliminated. Since the Postal Service is usually keen to deny that any such subsidies exist, it should not be worried about cream-skimming.

We have every reason to suspect, however, that the current rate structure of postal services contains significant cross-subsidies. These subsidies are difficult to track down, and require expeditions into the arcane world of rate structures. Consider, however, the Postal Service's use of the "Inverse Elasticity Rule" in the *National Association of Greeting Card Publishers* case. In that case, the USPS revealed that it uses a very generous standard in determining what is a "reasonably assignable" common cost. Costs incurred handling fourth class mail, for instance, are deemed common costs. These costs are then assessed against the various classes of mail, depending on the elasticity of demand for them. Since the demand for first class mail is the most inelastic, first class mailers end up bearing the lion's share of the "common cost" of handling fourth class mail. Subsidies also take place within classes of mail. These subsidies are also difficult to monitor and prevent, in large part because the Postal Service does not keep records which the executive branch, let alone the public, can examine to determine whether cross-subsidies are taking place. One wonders, however, if first class rates rose 60 percent more than second class rates between 1980 and the latest increase in part because the Postal Service has a monopoly in the former, but not the latter, type of mail. In the latest increase, second class rates will rise slightly more than first class rates, but in the fight against cross-subsidization the Postal Rate Commission has its work cut out for it.

The inefficient cross-subsidies buried in our postal rate structures require the protection of the private express statutes to survive. Why not, then, simply repeal the private express statutes, and let private firms enter the market with more efficient pricing policies? I will consider now some of the various objections that are made to repealing the postal monopoly laws altogether, and conclude by examining some other steps that could be taken to nibble away at the postal monopoly, if it cannot be eliminated altogether.

The first objection usually raised against repeal of the federal postal monopoly is that rural areas would cease getting mail service. In this form at least, the objection is clearly wrong. In a mail system in which the federal service had to compete with the private sector, all that would happen is that private firms could compete with the federal government's subsidized service. Repeal of the private express statutes could make clear that the Postal Service would not be obligated to provide service in an area if it could not compete with the prices or services of a private firm. Areas requiring subsidized mail in order to have any mail service at all could still get their subsidies. Explicit subsidies appropriated by Congress are much to be preferred to subsidies eked out of first class mailers on more profitable routes, however, because price distortions can be avoided.

If the policy of universal service is to be maintained, one must anticipate controversy around how much the Postal Service should charge for sending mail in and out of areas which private firms cannot profitably serve. The post office should charge at least as much as a private firm would have to, to serve such a market, and would probably have to charge more, since it is unlikely the Postal Service could serve these areas as efficiently as a private firm could. Even if cross-subsidies could be eliminated, the same forces that led to the initial expansion of the postal monopoly would tend to push Congress toward subsidizing public postal patrons so much that people might prefer the government's subsidized (but to them cheaper) Postal Service over that provided by the private sector. As long as the Postal Service can get money from Congress to make up for losses incurred in providing services not provided by the private sector, there will be strong pressure for the postal monopoly to spread out again, driving its competitors out with taxpayers' money. Even if there is no cream to skim, pork is still pork.

How can Congress be restrained from giving out subsidies that serve only to keep everyone within easy reach of a post office, without driving private firms out of business? Unfortunately, if the policy of guaranteed universal service by the Postal Service is maintained, many difficult pricing and monitoring problems will remain for the Postal Service and the Postal Rate Commission. These problems could be eliminated by absolving the Postal Service of the responsibility of providing universal service, but as the history of the Post Office suggests, this is the most sacred cow in the postal herd.

Experience argues, however, that private express firms competing with the Postal Service would have economic incentives to provide universal service. Both UPS and Federal Express began providing less-than-universal service, but moved to it as they realized their customers wanted the assurance that letters and parcels could reach anywhere in the country. No regulation requires this private universal service; it is produced by private-market incentives. Similarly, Sprint and MCI started off in the long-distance phone market providing service only to major cities, but quickly expanded to provide service virtually everywhere in the country.

Especially if universal service could be provided by market incentives and without public support, the social benefit from subsidizing the postal rates of rural locations is difficult to see. In the last great postal debate in the 1840s, defenders of the federal monopoly argued that without publicly provided postal service, the frontiers would revert to their savage state. Those who today venture to the outposts of Boulder, Colorado, or Juneau, Alaska, are more likely to have some more genteel form of that reversion precisely in mind. Requiring them to pay something closer to the cost of moving their mail is not about to lead to rebellion on the frontiers. Even if we suppose, however, that there is some social benefit from subsidizing the postal services of those who live in relatively expensive postal areas, providing this subsidy by charging high rates to other postal patrons is inefficient. If some patrons are to have their postal services subsidized, it should be done explicitly, so that the costs of the subsidy can be calculated and weighed against the benefits. Hiding the subsidies in the thicket of the rate structure, however, makes them very difficult to measure and evaluate, let alone remove.

Another objection raised to repealing the private express statutes is that competition would force the Postal Service to eliminate services valued by its customers, such as window service, daily delivery, and door-to-door service. Recently, however, many postal patrons have noted a deterioration in the quality of postal services, even without the rigors of competition. The Postal Service has cut back delivery schedules and decreed that newly constructed homes shall be equipped with cluster boxes, rather than the traditional box at the end of the driveway or next to the door. The Postal Service meets its own standards of delivery only 30 percent of the time for third class mail. In this atmosphere of apparently deteriorating service, increasing costs, and growing agitation by mail service users, the suggestion that competition would make matters worse is hard to believe. Quite to the contrary, competition implies the necessity to improve service.

Complete repeal of the private express statutes, allowing free entry into all aspects of the postal service business, may be impossible to attain politically. Several steps, however, could be taken to help clear the way for complete repeal. First, the governors of the Postal Service could redefine "letter" to exclude such types of mail as bills, receipts, statements of account, third class direct mail advertising matter, or even holiday greeting cards, leaving these to private firms.

Moreover, private firms could be allowed to deliver mail destined for or originating from rural areas. Currently, rural mail is, if anything, a subsidy-user, not a subsidy-generator. If private delivery companies could provide rural mail service more efficiently, it would save money for both the USPS and its customers.

Another possible step would be to expand the exception in the private express statutes for "extremely urgent" mail. Current regulations allow private companies to deliver express mail if the charge is at least $3 or 10 times the applicable postage, whichever is more, and if delivery is promised within 12 hours or by noon the next day for most geographical areas. This exception could be widened by lowering the allowable charge and by lengthening the allowed delivery time. One can imagine there would be a considerable market for a Federal Express–like service guaranteeing delivery of a letter within two or three days and charging $2 a letter. As important as prompt delivery is safe delivery. Informal discussions with heavy mail users in the financial industry suggest that the U.S. Postal Service's Express Mail is useless to them. Delivery times are unreliable, and, unlike private express companies, when the U.S. Postal Service loses an Express Mail item, it cannot easily be traced. Federal Express, by contrast, encodes each item with a numerical code, like that used in many grocery stores; in the event an item does not appear on time, it can be tracked down. Expanding the "extremely urgent" exception might well allow private firms to provide safe delivery to more customers who would be willing to buy it at less than the overnight-delivery price. Regulation could also be relaxed to allow part-time, not just full-time, employees to deliver mail within a firm.

The private express statutes not only prohibit private carriage and delivery of letters, they also prohibit depositing any item in an ordinary household mailbox, unless postage for the item has been paid. Revoking or narrowing this prohibition would be an important step toward privatization. For example, the statutory restriction could be narrowed so that it applied only to first and third class letters. The statutes do not prohibit private delivery of second class mail, which includes magazines, newspapers, and other periodicals, or fourth class mail, which includes merchandise, printed matter, and other parcels. A statute does prohibit delivering these items to mailboxes, however, making private delivery of many items more cumbersome.

Another modest step toward cutting back on the federal postal monopoly would be to allow charitable organizations to use mailboxes. For example, the local church could announce its annual Christmas play through fliers delivered to mailboxes.

All of the steps I have discussed are obviously incremental. I pose them because of the political difficulties with complete and immediate repeal of the private express statutes in their entirety, as appealing as that option is in many ways. The main problem with immediate repeal is, of course, the power of the postal unions. Postal services in this country today are much more labor-intensive than they would be in a competitive system, and postal employees are paid significantly more than equally skilled workers in the private sector. The Postal Service has lost the parcel post market to United Parcel Service, in part because of its refusal or inability to choose appropriate mixes of capital and labor. As one commentator put it as late as 1977:

> Despite the many advantages in fork-lift trucks and mechanized handling technology, the Post Office's chief accomplishment over the last 200 years has been limited to the introduction of durable, lightweight, colored nylon bags for use with airmail.

While the Postal Service was busy stuffing parcels into canvas bags that were basically the same as those used by the ancient Phoenicians to save "cube," or space, in the holds of their sailing vessels, UPS adopted modern containerization and mechanized handling technology. The Postal Service may have caught up some in the last ten years, but it still lags far behind the private sector in application of technology and in labor productivity. One is tempted to say that the Postal Service's reputation for constancy is better deserved for the technology that it uses than for delivering the mail in inclement weather.

I will not discuss here the various steps that could be taken to protect the rents the postal unions have managed to secure for themselves over the years. Some such plan may very well be the price we have to pay for privatizing the Postal Service. Given what we pay to maintain the monopoly, even a very generous settlement with the postal workers might well be worth the price. We should consider, however, what postal services might look like in the future if competition were allowed. The Commission on Privatization does a good job in describing the likely structure of a private postal industry.

One would expect there to be a mix of firms, some providing univeral or near-universal service, while other firms provided local delivery. These firms would probably form contractual arrangements with each other. One would expect a greater variety of specialized services to be available, and a greater number of places where mail could be dropped off. Liability for mail could be tracked by logging systems which would probably be much more sophisticated than anything the Postal Service is likely to adopt. Private expresses would probably compete for mailers with prices, promptness of delivery, and guarantees of safety. Contrary to what the governors have claimed, there is no reason the integrity of the mail could not be guaranteed by law, even in a private system. Indeed, given that sophisticated mailers now use private expresses not only for speed, but also to guarantee the safety of confidential documents and negotiable instruments, this is a particularly weak argument for the federal monopoly.

If postal services really are a natural monopoly, then one could expect one firm to emerge and dominate the market, and perhaps that firm would be a privatized version of today's Postal Service. More likely, however, would be a number of competing firms, since if anything the evidence indicates not natural monopoly, but the beginnings of a very competitive industry.

Against this rosy view of the private mail system of the future, I should also call to your attention a more cautionary, and perhaps more realistic, picture. The history of the postal monopoly should teach us that over the decades the Postal Service has been very successful in defending its turf. When competitors arose to challenge what the Post Office considered the core of its monopoly power—first class mail—it took the necessary steps to stamp out the competition with new laws and regulations. Perhaps the greatest threat to the federal monopoly of first class mail today is the ongoing technological revolution in telecommunications. We can easily imagine that in a decade or two, hard-copy first class mail will be as obsolete as mailing someone a note to ask them to tea the same afternoon. If technological developments begin to diminish the value of the Postal Service's monopoly, we would be historically naive to think it will stand idly by. In 1976, for example, the Postal Service proposed restrictions on checkless bill-paying through electronic transfers of funds. No paper was involved here, and no mailboxes. How could the Postal Service think they had the power to regulate such activities and, by implication, extract a rent when they occurred?

The Postal Service asserted this power on the basis of its extremely broad definition of a "letter." According to the Postal Service, any "message in or on a physical object sent to a specific address" is a letter. Moreover, there is nothing to stop the Postal Service from defining a "letter" even more broadly than this. The

Postal Service has promulgated exceptions to this broad definition which apply to many of the familiar forms of business communication. But as bills, receipts, and other routine business communications go electronic, the Postal Service will try to protect its rents, if history is any guide at all.

There is a relatively simple legislative solution to this problem. Congress should pass a law that prohibits the Postal Service from interpreting the private express statutes in any way that expands their application beyond their present scope. Through the legal doctrine of "reasoned elaboration," the governors of the Postal Service have asserted the power to expand upon the private express statutes and adopt enabling regulations. In a final touch seemingly calculated to make the legally scrupulous weep, the governors have also seized upon a codification error in an obscure postal statute to assert the power to grant exceptions to private express prohibitions as they think fit. This is a very useful tool to the monopolist as well, of course, because it allows the monopolist to grant exceptions to potential opponents of the monopoly, when necessary, to relieve the political pressure to get rid of it.

The arbitrary power the Postal Service now has to expand the private express prohibitions through regulation, and to placate opposition through ad hoc exemptions, presents a real threat to the future of the communications industry. If we cannot repeal the private express statutes, we should at least try to keep the Postal Service from expanding their application to include the technologies of the next century. As I have briefly tried to suggest in this paper, the federal postal monopoly is dynamic, not static. If technological progress is to free us from the outmoded postal monopoly, we must now take active steps to consign it to the past, or at least prevent it from following us into the future.

8. Why Marginal Reform of the U.S. Postal Service Won't Succeed

Douglas K. Adie

The Postal Service has quality-of-service, labor relations, financial, and innovational problems for which its patrons, its competitors, the taxpayers, and the government suffer. Most of these problems have been apparent for many years and have persisted through two organizational reforms. In the minds of some, they appear to have become even worse in the last few years.

Why do these problems exist? The question must be answered before any effective changes can be made; otherwise, changes that are made might not deal with the underlying causes of the problems. This article will attempt to set forth the basic motivations of the main participants and understand how, together, they have produced the present results. Once we understand the cause or causes of the problems, we then can consider what to do about them.

The array of policy alternatives has narrowed somewhat in the last few years, but they can be separated into two groups: marginal reforms and substantive reforms. It is my contention that marginal reforms, which preserve the government-owned monopoly, will not succeed in dealing adequately with the problems of the Postal Service. Finally, the article will illustrate how the Postal Service deals, or could deal, with its problems under different organizational structures, by considering labor relations problems and attempts to innovate.

The author is a professor of economics at Ohio University.

How the U.S. Postal Service Functions[1]

The Postal Service is a public corporation, but no citizens own tradeable shares through which they can exercise control over its operations. There is a responsibility and accountability vacuum because there is no adequate, legitimate means by which anyone can force the Postal Service to change its ways and become efficient. There is no incentive structure. Because the Postal Service is a public corporation, it does not function internally in the same manner as privately owned and operated corporations. In a privately owned corporation, when executives and managers make incorrect decisions or workers work slowly, produce inferior products or services, or are generally inefficient, the profitability of the company suffers. This reduces the potential income and security of both management and workers. The public is able to turn to better performing competitors providing the same services. The owners or shareholders, who may number in the millions, can express their dissatisfaction by selling some of their shares of common stock. This causes the market value of the shares of the poorly run company to fall.

By contrast, when Postal Service executives make incorrect decisions, or managers or workers produce inferior postal services, there is no straightforward mechanism by which this problem can be corrected. The income and security of the management and workers are guaranteed by public funds and the power of the post office lobby's political clout with Congress. The public cannot shift its business to more efficient competitors because competition is prohibited by law. Consequently, the gross inefficiency that resides within the Postal Service is not the result of the character or personality of the individuals who happen to hold the executive and managerial positions within the corporation. Rather, it stems from the nature of the incentive structure, institutional arrangements, and property rights within the service itself.

---

[1]The discussion of general principles in this chapter has benefited from Zane A. Spindler, "Bricking-Up Government Bureaus and Crown Corporations," in J. M. Ohashi and others, *Privatization: Theory and Practice* (Vancouver, B.C.: The Frazer Institute, 1980); Roger L. Miller, *Economics Today: The Micro View*, 6th ed. (New York: Harper & Row, 1988), pp. 124–25; and James Gwartney and Richard E. Wagner, "The Public Choice Revolution," *The Intercollegiate Review* 23, no. 2 (Spring 1988): 17–26.

How then does a public corporation like the Postal Service function? It functions, as Nobel Laureate Jim Buchanan, his colleague Gordon Tullock, or the many other developers of public choice theory would remind us, through a political process which is the set of interrelationships between the key players—citizens, executives, managers, unions, postal workers, politicians, the Postal Rate Commission, and postal governors. In particular, politicians are motivated by election victories; postal officials by the size of budget increases (especially the discretionary portion); and large patrons, which compose an interest group, by subsidized rates. Only the voters and private citizens are aloof from the process, because they do not spend a significant proportion of their budgets on twenty-five cent stamps. They care little about postal issues except at rate increase time, because they perceive that postal issues have little noticeable impact on their welfare. They are "rationally uninformed" because the time and energy necessary to examine postal issues and compute their impact costs more than it's worth. Remote rural residents, who depend more on postal service for a physical communication link, will be more concerned but not necessarily better informed.

In this framework, what happens within the Postal Service? Since the self-interest of a public corporation's bureaucrats is so clearly connected to the size of the corporation's budget, the proximate goal of the Postal Service is budget maximization, especially that portion which is discretionary, as William Niskanen has suggested.[2] A larger discretionary budget contributes to fulfilling basic motives of the participants because it enhances the opportunities and resources available throughout the Postal Service by expanding power, prestige, salary, and other benefits to managers, executives, and governors. A larger discretionary budget offers additional job security, promotional opportunities, and potential salary and wage increases for managers and postal workers. Larger discretionary budgets also permit more office space, furniture, travel, and other resources that make the work environment more pleasant. So postal workers, unions, managers, executives, and governors, and even

[2]William Niskanen, *Bureaucracy and Representative Government* (Chicago: Aldine-Atherton, 1970); also, Gordon Tullock, *The Vote Motive* (London: The Institute of Economic Affairs, 1976), ch. IV.

the rate commissioners, unite behind a strategy to increase the Postal Service budget.

On the basis of the budget-maximizing decision rule, the Postal Service overproduces total output, utilizing more resources than it ought to, and therefore misuses resources. The net value to society of output produced by a government enterprise such as the Postal Service is less than that produced by a private enterprise such as a private postal company. The difference in the values, with both using the same resources, is social cost. The social cost of the U.S. Postal Service is about $17 billion annually.[3] For this cost, society receives a change in the distribution of goods and services.

How is this change in distribution brought about and what does it look like? The Postal Service, like other public corporations, discriminates by plundering one group for the benefit of another, in many different ways, including use of pricing policy and budget allocations. Instead of using resources for the socially beneficial purposes of delivering the mail faster, cheaper, and more reliably, their efforts are directed to the redistribution of previously created wealth from first class mailers to users of other classes, from urban to rural residents, from other workers to postal workers, and from other goods and services to postal services. To effect the last-named transfer, the Board of Governors, executives, unions, and postal workers lobby Congress to preserve the private express statutes, which are used to ban competitors and even prevent private citizens from delivering their own first class mail without paying postage. To add insult to injury, this rent-seeking lobbying is paid for with real resources which could otherwise have been used to produce real goods and services.

---

[3]Madison Pirie, *Dismantling the State*, (Dallas, Tex.: National Center for Policy Analysis, 1985), pp. 8–53. Pirie says that costs of production in U.S. private industry are 40 percent lower than in the public sector. He also says that when the activities are contracted out, while the responsibility for the provision of services remains with the government, immediate savings are normally in the 20 to 40 percent range. The addition of the fact that postal employees are one-third overpaid suggests that a 50 percent savings from privatization would not be unreasonable. Also, Robert Poole, "Privatization from the Bottom Up," in *Privatization*, ed. John C. Goodman (Dallas, Tex.: National Center for Policy Analysis, 1985), pp. 66–67. Poole says that private air traffic controllers can do the job for half the cost of the publicly managed air traffic controllers.

Present postal policy is the result of the power of special interests rather than sound economic analysis. Postal policy such as the private express statutes drains our resources, diminishes our welfare, and infringes on our liberties. While this policy affects the visible costs of the average citizen only slightly, it indirectly affects the costs of many other goods and services and, perhaps even more important, the way we communicate. The defects of a government-owned and -operated enterprise are lack of accountability; inefficiency of operations; excessive wages, salaries, and benefits for employees and managers; misappropriation of resources; excessive output; loss in net value to society; and a maldistribution of economic benefits. All are present to some degree with the Postal Service.

Astute politicians could correct these matters easily if it were not for intense lobbying by special interest groups. Since the personal stake of the beneficiaries—namely, the postal governors, executives, workers, unions, and large patrons—is substantial, they inform themselves thoroughly and let legislators know how they feel and will vote. They support politicians who support them, with funds and effort, and oppose those who do not. Vote-seeking politicians, who gain little from supporting the interests of the largely uninformed and disinterested majority, heed the special interests which provide votes, campaign workers, and contributions to help to win the support of others. The Postal Service can also marshal some of its large patrons to attempt to influence the legislative process. For instance, Melvin Laird, a member of the President's Commission on Privatization, who is also on the board of directors of the *Reader's Digest*, a large postal patron, opposed holding hearings on the Postal Service—albeit unsuccessfully.

To make the job of reform more difficult, the major, if not the sole, source of information on the Postal Service's performance is a biased source—the Postal Service itself—that uses this information (and disinformation) to influence legislation and public opinion. For instance, the Postal Service controls the use of its service performance index (measuring speed and reliability of delivery) in such a way as to give postal managers more leeway to cover inefficiencies and pursue personal objectives. Such factors reduce the ability of the executive branch and legislative committees to control postal costs. Even the threat of bankruptcy is no real problem to the Postal

Service; instead of being a prod to efficiency, such a possibility merely generates pressure for larger government appropriations or rate hikes.

The fault in this system lies not with the character of postal employees, who are no less energetic, competent, or committed to their work than others, but with the organizational structure. Postal Service performance depends importantly on how its operating rules influence the incentives of the governors, executives, managers, and workers, not on who in particular happens to hold office. The incentive structure under which postal employees work predicts the behavior we see and the many examples of inefficiency. If the Postal Service were functioning properly, its efficiency would not depend, as it does now, on the benevolence of its participants, but on a well-constructed order that would channel the pursuit of self-interest into socially desirable directions, as would be the case in a privately owned postal service subject to competition.

What is Marginal Reform?

Marginal reform is any organizational change that leaves intact the basic motivational system within the Postal Service. A few marginal reforms have been suggested as possible remedies for the current situation. The possibilities include increasing the surveillance powers of Congress, the president, the board of governors, and/or the Postal Rate Commission; installing better managers; or relying more on contracting out postal services to private businesses.

Contracting out is the most serious proposal among the marginal reforms. Its most outspoken advocate is John W. Crutcher, vice chairman of the Postal Rate Commission, who recommends that postal functions be contracted out to private businesses while keeping the managerial functions of the Postal Service intact.[4] Crutcher

[4]See John W. Crutcher, "Privatizing the U.S. Postal Service," *Vital Speeches* 50, no. 1 (October 15, 1983): 29–32; "The Privatization of the Postal Service," *Washington Times*, June 2, 1983; "Remarks at the First National Conference on Privatization Opportunities," New York City, June 29, 1986 (unpublished manuscript).

See also Stephen Moore, "Privatizing the U.S. Postal Service," ch. 2, *Privatization: A Strategy for Taming the Federal Budget: Fiscal Year 1987*, eds. Stephen Moore and Stewart M. Butler (Washington, D.C.: Heritage Foundation, 1987). In 1980 the Heritage Foundation questioned the need for a publicly owned and supported national document delivery company. *Mandate for Leadership* project team report for

points out that under the current legal framework, the Postal Service could operate more efficiently by contracting out to private companies large segments of its operations, such as rural delivery.[5] At present the Postal Service contracts with private carriers to transport mail; with entrepreneurs to run postal stations; with star carriers to deliver mail; and with presorters, who receive a discount to provide sorting service. It might be pointed out that contracting out increases the discretionary part of the Postal Service's remaining budget. For this reason, it is a policy supported by most participants, except for the postal unions.

The improvements to efficiency from contracting out spring from a realization that the USPS, a government corporation with little accountability, is unable to supervise, monitor, reward, and discipline its employees adequately, so as to produce a reasonably efficient operation. A private business, which can appropriate the residual, is better able to do this and share its profits with the USPS. Contracting out does lead to greater efficiency of operations, but only in those parts that are contracted out. It provides the remaining managerial structure of the Postal Service with discretionary income, enabling managers to pursue self-serving activities to a greater extent.

Would this policy contribute to long-run overall efficiency? I doubt very much that the Postal Service would use the gains from these efficiency measures in any other way than they have in the past—namely, to increase salaries and operate less efficiently in other areas or even to finance graft or kickbacks. These results are

---

the U.S. Postal Service and Postal Rate Commission (draft) (Heritage Foundation, 1980), pp. 22–23, 30. More recently, however, the Heritage Foundation has backed away from this substantive reform and advocates instead that the USPS be converted into an umbrella organization responsible for postal service. It recommends, "Many of the actual services be provided by private sector contractors on a competitive basis . . . USPS would . . . turn over operation of its collection, sorting, transportation, and distribution functions to private firms on a contract basis." Carlos E. Bonilla, "Postal System," *Agenda 1983: A Mandate for Leadership Report,* ed. Richard N. Holwill (Heritage Foundation, 1983), p. 353. This amounts to only marginal reform as it leaves the government-owned monopoly intact.

[5]Phil Crane, Republican congressman from Illinois, said that private carriers deliver rural routes at one-third the cost to the Postal Service and still make a profit. Philip Crane, "Privatize the Post Office through Employee Ownership," *Congressional Record,* April 30, 1987, E1670.

not accidents of the present system but are endemic to it.[6] Under the present organizational form there is a lack of incentive for the Postal Service to operate efficiently. When it receives gains from contracting out, why should it pass those gains on to customers in the form of lower rates, or to taxpayers in the form of lower subsidies from the federal government, or a reduction in tax concessions? There is no appropriate incentive for the managers to use the savings from contracting out in the public's interest. While providing some temporary savings to the Postal Service, contracting out does not offer much promise for the future. I agree with Bert Ely when

[6]For instance, Peter Voss, a former governor of the Postal Service, pleaded guilty May 30, 1986, to accepting more than $20,000 in illegal payments from a Michigan-based public relations firm as part of a plan to steer $250 million worth of agency contracts to a Dallas-based manufacturer named Recognition Equipment, Inc. (REI). Former postmaster general Paul Carlin claimed in an affidavit that, beginning in January 1985, he was pressured by Mr. Voss and another postal board governor, Ruth Peters, to make decisions favoring REI. Three former senior agency officials were convicted in early 1988 for participation in the multimillion dollar kickback and bribery scheme. In April 1987, the governors limited the independent Postal Inspection Service's access to tapes of closed board meetings which were needed to probe the Voss scandal. The Postal Inspection Service in also investigating possible insider trading in the stock of REI, the bidder for the mail-sorting equipment contracts. A surge in REI stock trading occurred immediately after the closed door meetings of the Postal Service Board of Governors, where policy changes enhancing REI's chances of landing a lucrative contract were discussed. Jeanne Saddler, "Postal Official Was Asked to Quit Post as Agency Tried to Deal with Scandal," *Wall Street Journal*, June 27, 1986, p. 12; "Ex-Postal Chief Sues Service to Get Job Back," *Wall Street Journal*, July 1, 1986, p. 19. Bruce Ingersoll, "Postal Unit Probes Trading Activity of Firm's Stock," *Wall Street Journal*, July 3, 1986, p. 34.

When Albert V. Casey became postmaster general, he gave his old friend and Harvard Business School classmate, John T. Garrity, a no-bid contract for $900 per day to advise the U.S. Postal Service on a major reorganization, under which Garrity was paid $156,000 over the next 7½ months. As if this was not enough, in November 1986 Casey gave him another no-bid contract to evaluate the recommendations he made under the first contract. Up to the middle of May 1987 Garrity had received $117,000 under this contract. The next postmaster general, Preston Tisch, continued Garrity's $900 rate even if he worked as little as one hour a day. Sen. David H. Pryor, chairman of a Senate Governmental Affairs subcommittee, asked Postmaster General Preston R. Tisch to cancel Garrity's contract. Pryor said it was "bad enough" for Garrity to be paid $156,000 in salary and $14,000 in expenses for work that was actually done by a dozen or so senior postal officials, but that it "borders on the outrageous" for Garrity to be rehired so he can "pat himself on the back" for his earlier recommendations. Howard Kurtz, "At USPS, a $900-a-Day Consultant," *Washington Post*, May 13, 1987, p. A21.

he indicates that only in comparison with the Postal Service's current mode of operation as a rigid, bureaucratic, publicly owned business does contracting out represent efficiency gains.

Moreover, contracting out creates a new interest group that will support the status quo against substantive reform. This group comprises the private contractors who currently have contracts with the Postal Service. They will oppose privatization simply to protect their current arrangements, which guarantee them income. Union contractors and suppliers who specialize in serving the Postal Service fear losing their highly valued relationships. Some of the airlines that contract to deliver mail for the Postal Service might also oppose privatization if they feared their relationship would be jeopardized; this might be the case if the Postal Service or a divested division planned to provide national hub service itself. At present much of the intercity mail is moved by 11,000 independent truckers operating under contract with the Postal Service. A private postal company might find it more desirable to operate its own trucks with its own employees—or even to operate some of its own aircraft, as Federal Express and UPS do. Organizational changes at least put in jeopardy these contracts and for this reason contract truckers might object to privatization. Such opposition could be reduced by not expanding, or even reducing, the contracting out program at this time, while the Postal Service is still government owned.

What is Substantive Reform?

Substantive reform involves, at the very least, deregulation and privatization, and preferably also divestiture of the Postal Service. The most important part of deregulation is repeal of the private express statutes. The key element of privatization is the transfer of ownership and control of the U.S. Postal Service from the public to the private sector. The divestiture that I have proposed elsewhere involves dividing the Postal Service into five regional delivery systems, a clearinghouse and support services company, and a bulk mail company.[7]

Former Rep. Philip M. Crane, Christopher Elias, Daniel Oliver, Robert Poole, Bert Ely, International Resource Development, Inc.,

---

[7]Douglas K. Adie, "Getting the Postal Service to Deliver: Privatization Would Work," *Wall Street Journal*, March 31, 1988, p. 22.

the *New York Times*, and the President's Commission on Privatization suggested transferring ownership and control of the U.S. Postal Service from the public to the private sector.[8] Members of the Board of Postal Governors, who have authority to make postal policy, were singularly mute. Postal governors allow private companies to carry only a very limited amount of first class material, under very tight restrictions. The governors could narrow the definition of the private express statutes to reduce the Postal Service's monopoly, grant waivers from the statutes for certain geographical areas or types of mail, or even repeal the statutes, but we have not heard any serious discussion from them on this topic.

John L. Ryan, currently vice chairman of the Board of Governors, was an outspoken critic of the Postal Service before his appointment. As a member of President Reagan's transition team, he even advocated repealing the private express statutes. After becoming a governor, when he was in a position to suspend the statutes, he was silent.

John R. McKeon, former chairman of the Board of Governors and another Reagan appointee, admitted that the Postal Service is not serving consumers well. Journalist Doug Bandow challenged McKeon and the other governors, if they are sincere about wanting to serve the interests of customers, to suspend enforcement of the monopoly provisions.[9] There was no response.

The policy I advocate here is not ideologically based, but is rooted in public welfare. The governors' resistance is likewise not ideological, but is rooted in their vested interest, even though some of them have expressed views of liberty in direct conflict with their postal positions.

[8]Rep. Philip M. Crane, "Privatize the Post Office through Employee Ownership," *Congressional Record*, April 30, 1987, E1669-1671. Christopher Elias, "Would Privatization Make Postal Service Letter-Perfect?" *Insight*, July 6, 1987, pp. 42–44. Daniel Oliver, chairman, Federal Trade Commission, "Saving the Post Office," before the Direct Marketing Association's Government Affairs Conference, Loews L'Enfant Plaza Hotel, Washington, D.C., May 15, 1987, pp. 3, 4, 6, 8. Robert Poole, "Is This Any Way to Run a Postal Service? No," *Wall Street Journal*, October 11, 1982. "Teleprinting and Electronic Mail," International Resource Development Inc., Norwalk, Conn., May 15, 1985. "Move the Mail, or the Postal Service," *New York Times*, June 16, 1986, Editorial section.

[9]Doug Bandow, "Postal Service Doesn't Deserve Monopoly," *Los Angeles Times*, July 2, 1986, Part II.

Problems with Labor Relations

Since reorganization, Postal Service management has had sole responsibility for decisions concerning new facilities, operations, and personnel policies. Many people have argued, however, that despite giving management the responsibility, the Postal Reorganization Act failed to give them enough motivation to pursue the risk of bringing efficiency measures into the Postal Service.

The most glaring example of inefficiency may be the level of postal wages. Postal labor costs are approximately 83 percent of total costs. This is extremely high relative to other companies, even those in service industries. Like others who have examined the level of wages, I have found Postal Service wages to be excessive by approximately one-third compared to what the service would need to pay to attract and hold a competent work force, or what postal workers would get, given their experience and education, if they were employed elsewhere.[10] How did this inequity occur? Has

[10]Joel L. Fleishman, ed., *The Future of the Postal Service*, published with the Aspen Institute for Humanistic Studies (New York: Praeger, 1983), p. 12, fn. 31. Douglas K. Adie, "How Have Postal Workers Fared Since the 1970 Act?" in *Perspectives on Postal Service Issues*, Roger Sherman, ed. (Washington, D.C.: American Enterprise Institute, 1980), pp. 74–93. Commentary by Sharon P. Smith, pp. 94–98, and Discussion, pp. 99–107. Douglas K. Adie, *An Evaluation of Postal Service Wage Rates* (Washington, D.C.: American Enterprise Institute, 1977). Review of this book by Sharon P. Smith, "Review of Labor Market," *Industrial and Labor Relations Review, An Evaluation of Postal Service Wage Rates*, October 1978, pp. 122–23, and her book *Equal Pay in the Public Sector: Fact or Fantasy?* Research Report Series no. 122, Industrial Relations Section (Princeton University, 1977); Sharon P. Smith, "Are Postal Workers Over or Underpaid?" *Industrial Relation* 15, no. 2 (May 1976).

For a study commissioned by the Postal Service, see Michael L. Wachter and Jeffrey M. Perloff, "An Evaluation of U.S. Postal Service Wages," University of Pennsylvania Discussion Paper, July 15, 1981. Also, Jeffrey M. Perloff and Michael L. Wachter, "Wage Comparability in the U.S. Postal Service," *Industrial and Labor Relations Review* 38, no. 1 (October 1984) (under contract with U.S. Postal Service during 1981 negotiations). Martin Asher and Joel Popkin, "The Effect of Gender and Race Differentials on Public-Private Wage Comparisons: A Study of Postal Workers," *Industrial and Labor Relations Review* 38, no. 1 (October 1984) (under contract to APWU and NALC during 1981 negotiations). Also Michael L. Wachter and Jeffrey M. Perloff, "U.S. Postal Service Economic Presentation," July 15, 1981, manuscript, unpaginated.

Jeff Perloff and I acknowledged unanimity of conclusions in our testimony in hearings before the Subcommittee on Economic Goals and Intergovernmental Policy of the Joint Economic Committee, Congress of the United States, Ninety-seventh Congress, Second Session, June 18 and 21, 1982, called *The Future of Mail Delivery in the United States*, pp. 282–99, 299–313, 323–24. For a general treatment of the literature discussing and evaluating postal worker wages, see Alan L. Sorkin, *The Economics of the Postal System*, (Lexington, Mass.: Lexington Books, 1980), pp. 73–78, 85.

there been a change in the labor relations climate permitting a correction? More important, is there any hope for redressing the inequity on excessive wages short of substantive reform?

Murray Comarow, former senior assistant postmaster general for customer service recalled that former postmaster general "Klassen was under attack by everyone. He didn't have a friend in the world and he bought friends. He gave the unions everything they wanted."[11] Benjamin Bailar, another former postmaster general, was even more generous in the 1975 labor negotiations than Klassen.

Former postmaster general William F. Bolger has been called the most anti-labor postmaster general in history, despite his being a 37-year postal veteran. Moe Billar quotes Bolger as saying, "Frankly, if under the law I didn't have to have unions, I wouldn't." The climate of opinion in recent years has leaned more towards those Postal Service managers who tried to hold the line against postal unions' demands for wage increases. This changing climate and increased public awareness have enabled the Postal Service to take a much more aggressive position in bargaining. Bolger tried to capitalize on this in the 1984 negotiations.

When negotiations broke down, Bolger imposed a two-tiered wage structure for postal employees. Current employees remained on the same schedule they had been on, while new employees were brought in on a schedule which was 23 percent lower. This bold policy attempt, if continued, would have greatly reduced the excessive postal wages. Union leaders objected to the new wage structure. Terms of the reorganization had stipulated that an arbitration panel would deal with matters contested in the negotiations. Without waiting for the panel's decision, the unions appealed to Congress, which responded by imposing the following ultimatum on postal managers: if postal management didn't abolish the two-tiered wage schedule, Congress would refuse to continue its subsidies to the Postal Service.[12] In effect, this congressional intervention

[11]Kathleen Conkey, *The Postal Precipice, Can the U.S. Postal Service be Saved?* (Washington, D.C.: Center for the Study of Responsive Laws, 1983), pp. 149–50. Conkey's book is useful for tracing discussions on postal matters.

[12]In my opinion, postal managers should have maintained the two-tiered structure and accepted the abolition of the subsidy. They could have made whatever cost-cutting adjustments they found necessary to compensate for the loss of subsidy.

brought the Postal Service back into the political arena from which it tried to escape in the reorganization, and seriously hampered the postal managers' ability to function.

Before the 1987 contract expired, Deputy Postmaster General Michael Coughlin told the House Post Office Committee that management was seeking the right to hire more part-time employees to work at peak periods for lower wages. Rep. Frank McCloskey, the only member who responded, warned cryptically that it would be "unwise and shortsighted" to hire more part-timers. Perhaps intimidated, postal negotiators backed off pushing for more part-timers.

Despite the sobering results of the 1981 air traffic controllers' strike and the newfound restraint exercised by postal unions in bargaining, the effects on the outcome have been only marginal because of the arbitration process and congressional interference. As I predicted in 1977, unions quickly learned how to use this process to their advantage to obtain better contract terms for their members.[13] The evidence to date indicates that arbitration is ineffective in redressing the inequity of excessive wages. Nothing short of substantive reform will suffice.

The postal monopoly makes it impossible for postal managers to control their labor costs; lack of competition shields them from the necessity of pressing for economical wage settlements. Increased costs can always be financed by milking the "cash cows" of first class postage. Under competition, on the other hand, the Postal Service would not be able to pass along increased costs to its users without suffering severe deterioration of volume and market share. This—and perhaps nothing less—would constrain postal workers' wage demands.

Under 39 U.S.C. Sec. 3627, the Postal Service would have had the right to adjust the preferred rates upward to recapture lost income since the greatest part of the subsidies in 1984 and since has consisted of subsidies to preferred-rate mailers. The managers, however, did not buck Congress.

[13]Douglas K. Adie, *An Evaluation of Postal Service Wage Rates*, pp. 41, 62–63. The process by which the binding arbitration board is selected is as follows: The Federal Mediation and Conciliation Service submits a list of "neutral and impartial persons" to labor and management representatives from which each chooses one representative. The two representatives so selected choose a third person to serve as chairman. This process in the past has worked out in such a way as to favor labor.

To correct labor relations problems, substantive reform is necessary. Former PRC chairman A. Lee Fritschler said, concerning the Postal Service: "It's a monopoly, the unions are tough, the public does not look over their shoulder. It's a classical monopoly situation and it's not successfully regulated. . . . You're not going to find [postal] workers cutting their pay back the way the automotive workers are going to have to. The auto workers know that either they cut back or they don't have a job. The handwriting is clearly on the wall. That's not going to happen in monopoly industries."[14]

Chronic inefficiency in the USPS raises a series of questions. Is there consistent petty sabotage on the part of the employees in an attempt to protect jobs?[15] Is there a laxity in management's demands for performance? Or is there just a jinx on the USPS that allows them to take a perfectly sound idea and see it fall way short of its potential? Whatever the reason, a restructuring of USPS as a private, profit-making business would introduce enough incentives for management to find out what the problems are and solve them—or else themselves be removed.

Although reorganization was supposed to increase management's ability to conduct wage negotiations more favorable to the interests of patrons and taxpayers, that clearly didn't happen. The experience prompts the question, "Does the existing organizational structure provide management with the incentive to negotiate in the public's interest with the postal workers and unions?" The answer is a resounding "No!"

Under privatization, the labor relations situation could change drastically and quickly. Madsen Pirie, an experienced champion of

[14]Conkey, p. 265.

[15]A consistent policy of petty sabotage cannot be ruled out in the case of Canada Post. In 1968, when Canada's then–postmaster general Eric Kierans initiated a program of mechanization and modern managerial control, the Canadian Union of Postal Workers responded with a public statement concluding: "We, therefore, declare that unless the above reasonable and just conditions are met by our employer, we shall insure that the enormously expensive and complex mechanization program in the Post Office WILL NOT SUCCEED." (Emphasis in the original) L. M. Read in his study suggests that the CUPW has kept its promise. L. M. Read, "Canada Post: A Case Study in the Correlation of Collective Will and Productivity," in *Research on Productivity of Relevance to Canada,* Donald J. Daly, ed. (Ottawa: Social Science Federation of Canada, 1983), p. 131. Other questions to ask are what conditions allowed this situation to persist and what can be done about it?

privatization in Britain, cites the case of a state-owned trucking company which the government sold to its workers. The sale produced a change in the workers' attitudes towards their jobs and employer that was nothing short of astounding. Pirie says, "The workers, many of whom had mortgaged their houses and pooled their savings to buy the stock in the company, suddenly were no longer concerned about who does what and what their rights were. They were concerned about making money. . . . We had expected that over time it would move toward profitability. We had not expected it to do so on the first day, which is what happened."[16] This example describes the way changed incentives can work in favor of efficiency.

In a private postal company operating under competitive conditions, even without worker-owners, both unions and management have strong incentives to avoid strikes, work stoppages, slow-downs, or any diminution in service for the following reason: any of these disruptions will cause customers to shift their purchases of document delivery services to other competing carriers who, under repeal of the private express statutes, will be eager to take advantage of the situation. If workers want job security and employers want to retain market share, they will not just prevent work stoppages, they will work together to improve reliability of service.

Problems with Innovating

Appropriate responses to rapid changes in economic and technological conditions require innovative firms which respond to competitive pressures. Some have supported Postal Service deregulation as a means to encourage the competitive conditions that foster innovation. Large, government-protected monopolies, providing a service with few close substitutes, do not have the incentive to innovate in the provision of new services or to improve the quality of existing services, or to innovate in the use of new and improved equipment to produce existing services at lower cost, if they are unable to appropriate the residual. Instead, they will direct their efforts to preserving capital values by preventing other firms from entering and even by retarding innovations. For the Postal Service, this strategy is cheaper and less risky.

[16]Vaughn Palmer, "Incentive Is the Key to Privatization," *Vancouver Sun*, March 9, 1987.

In the telecommunications industry, before the breakup, AT&T was an example of this phenomenon. Knowledge and information expanded so rapidly that AT&T couldn't assemble, contain, and utilize it. Also, AT&T did not have a strong enough incentive to do this. Despite the fact that AT&T was a profit-making business, its virtual monopoly, where rates and profits were regulated, did not provide enough motivation for AT&T to implement existing technology as rapidly as it was developing. Instead, planning within AT&T became devoted to preserving capital values and even to retarding innovation.

The USPS is insulated from normal business risk in yet another way because its annual deficit is covered by an appropriation from the government. This insurance protects permanent workers from layoffs and also protects management from having to make tough internal decisions on the use of resources, and together with the monopoly of first class mail, provides an artificial environment where good business decisions are not encouraged. This may help to explain the fact that while there have been numerous technological innovations applicable to the postal service industry in the last 50 years, they have not been incorporated very effectively into the U.S. Postal Service. Successful innovation requires good business decisions, and these are more likely to be made in a competitive environment.

When the Postal Service did take advantage of new technology, as in the use of letter-sorting machines, the gains from the use of these machines were not passed on to customers as lower postage rates or to the public by a cessation of any subsidies. Rather, they too have been squandered on other inefficiencies, including wage increases for existing employees, featherbedding, increased employment, or graft.[17]

The USPS did innovate in providing new services such as a new parcel post network, overnight delivery, E-Com, nine-digit ZIP Code, new equipment, and an overseas instant communication system called INTELPOST. But have these innovations been successful? The volume of parcels handled by the Postal Service

[17]For a discussion of this thesis, see Douglas K. Adie, *Monopoly Mail: Privatizing the United States Postal Service* (New Brunswick, N.J.: Transaction, 1988).

between 1951 and 1974 fell over 50 percent. (A reason for this may be that the USPS, as reported by an internal survey, damaged half the packages marked "fragile.") Instead of focusing on the problem of package handling, Postmaster Winston Blount announced the building of a National Bulk Mail System in March 1971.

In five years, Postmaster Klassen built a bulk mail system around 21 major and 12 auxiliary regional bulk mail facilities, at a cost of nearly $2 billion. Each bulk mail center is in a centralized location and is equipped with expensive and elaborate machinery for processing all bulk mail originating from or coming into its area. The Postal Service sorts and processes all bulk mail, including parcels, circulars, advertisements, and some magazines, at these centers, which are separate from facilities used for first class mail. Despite the huge expenditure on the bulk mail network, the USPS failed to recapture the lost parcel post business. Fourteen years after the first USPS bulk mail center was opened in Jersey Meadows in 1974, UPS was carrying 90 percent of all parcels. Originally promoted as a cost-cutter, the National Bulk Mail System turned into a $1.5 billion financial albatross.

E-COM is another Postal Service experience with innovation which runs parallel to its bulk mail experience. E-COM is an electronic, computer-originated mail system which, despite legal prohibitions, was heavily subsidized. While originally costing a customer only $0.26 per letter, the Postal Service lost $5.25 on each E-COM letter the first year, and it continued to lose over $1.00 per letter until its termination. The USPS confirmed this failure by announcing in 1985 that it would shut down E-COM and look for a buyer.[18]

INTELPOST, an electronic mail service that sends instantaneous facsimile copies between continents, is another example of what appeared on the surface to be a good idea but was unsuccessfully executed by postal managers. The market proved to be much smaller than projected, and service was unreliable. There was a lack of consumer support, and this venture failed, too.

ZIP + 4, another example of the Postal Service's attempt to innovate, is a nine-digit ZIP Code system which permits a greater degree

[18]"Postal Service May Close Its Electronic Mail Service," *Wall Street Journal*, June 7, 1985, p. 14.

of mechanized sorting and, in the right hands, could cut labor costs dramatically. The Postal Service requested $900 million to implement ZIP + 4, but now says it does not have enough ZIP + 4 coded mail to make it worth sorting.[19] On the other hand, the reason the Postal Service does not have more ZIP + 4 mail may be because it does not offer enough of a discount to presorters of this mail to encourage its use.[20]

The Postal Service has not demonstrated competence in planning, carrying out, or marketing electronic services in a competitive and unregulated environment.[21] Indeed, the Postal Service has not learned much from any of its mistakes and apparently is plagued with the "Midas Touch in Reverse."[22] A pattern of failures in innovations that should have succeeded does not bode well for the future of the Postal Service in its present organizational form as it faces competition in a rapidly developing communications industry. Experience to date should raise a warning flag to both postal management and employees that the Postal Service needs a new form of organization that can cope and respond in today's rapidly paced communications industry. Can the United States Postal Service do a better job without substantive reforms? I doubt it. Why? Because the incentive system in place now predicts this outcome.

In 1969, Rep. Morris K. Udall, a member of the House Post Office Committee, said concerning the lack of technological advancement in the Postal Service, "I want to make very clear, I do not blame postal employees. I think we have fine dedicated people working

[19]See The President's Commission on Privatization Report, p. 104.

[20]In dealing with the Postal Service one quickly reaches a quandry and becomes exasperated. If ZIP + 4 is not cost effective at any volume, as it may appear, certainly the USPS's failure to provide incentives for using it is not grounds for criticism; but in this case their requesting $900 million is. However, if it would be cost effective at higher volume levels, failure to increase volume through the use of incentives is grounds for criticism.

[21]"INTELPOST: A Postal Service Failure in International Electronic Mail" (Washington, D.C.: House Government Operations Committee, April 11, 1984), p. 9.

[22]"The Midas Touch in Reverse" refers to the Postal Service's uncanny ability to take what appears to be a perfectly good idea and under the most favorable circumstances destroy its effectiveness through incompetence and bungling.

90

for us. I do not blame those who have undertaken to manage it in the past. I blame the system."[23]

To survive, the Postal Service needs a plan to introduce new services to replace revenues in declining markets. This strategy, however, requires not just managerial skills and entrepreneurial abilities (that do not normally surface in nationalized businesses), but also the freedom and incentive to make the necessary changes. The USPS and most public corporations have a poor record at innovating. Indeed, it is doubtful whether any innovations can make the USPS's operation substantially more efficient on an overall basis. If some phase of the business is made more efficient through innovation, the tendency is to "waste" the savings elsewhere in higher wages and salaries or reduced performance pressure. Since profits cannot be directly appropriated and the USPS is unlikely to propose rate reductions for first class mail, there are no other alternatives. However, this deficiency places the Postal Service at a substantial disadvantage in its ability to adapt to changing circumstances and should be corrected by the postal policy of divestiture, privatization, and deregulation.

Postal employees should not be held responsible for this deficiency. The motivational system existing under the current organization makes any other result unlikely. The qualities which are necessary to engage in risk-taking activities are honed under conditions where those responsible for making decisions suffer the losses from their mistakes or enjoy the gains from their successes. Those conditions would apply to the Postal Service only if it became a private business. Protectionism is a poor substitute for managerial effort, but represents the direction the Postal Service has invariably taken in the past when faced with difficulties.

In 1980, the communications equipment industry spent 5.2 percent of its net sales on research and development; the office, computing, and accounting machines industry spent 10 percent. In 1981, the Postal Service spent one-tenth of 1 percent of its total sales on research and development. The research and development program of the Postal Service lacks management support, adequate funding, and competent scientists and engineers. In 1988, the USPS

[23]*Post Office Reorganization* (Part I): Hearings before the House Committee on Post Office and Civil Service, Serial no. 91-93, 1969, p. 26, quoted in Conkey, p. 264.

slashed its already low capital spending budget for the next 21 months by $1.7 billion, which promised to slow down further its already-snail's-pace move toward mechanization.[24] Under the present organizational structure this may not be a bad strategy, since it does not put public money at risk.

The lesson which experience in the airline, telephone, transportation, steel, and auto industries teaches us is that the decisions needed to revitalize an industry and make it efficient result only under the threat of extinction which could occur with full-fledged competition. The competitive marketplace is the only effective regulator of economic activity. Through a process of trial and error, the market determines the most efficient way for producers to provide goods and services to consumers. The developments in the deregulated airline industry vividly demonstrate this view. Haranguing postal managers to be innovative, hard-nosed, and enterprising in their decisions is futile. This doesn't happen in the private sector in the absence of competition, so why should a government-owned corporation with many more obstacles be expected to respond any better?

[24]"Postal Service to Close Offices a Half Day a Week," *Wall Street Journal*, January 19, 1988, p. 1.

9. A Call for Private Third Class Mail Delivery: The Rationale

Gene A. Del Polito

Third class mail is used predominantly for three basic purposes: (1) to distribute printed advertising to generate in-store retail purchases of goods and services, (2) to generate a direct response, usually by mail, to solicitations to sell and market goods or services, and (3) to raise funds for charitable, religious, philanthropic, scientific, educational, and political purposes. To an extent, third class mail also serves for some nonprofit organizations as a nonmarketing communications medium (e.g., the distribution of magazines and newspapers and church bulletins), but for the most part, third class mail is used for the distribution of advertising and marketing information.

As an advertising and marketing tool, mail is an especially powerful medium. It enables advertisers and marketers to distribute messages in a broadcast fashion across a wide geographic area, or to target the distribution of messages selectively according to certain desired demographic or psychographic characteristics. In fact, mail is the only medium that has the power to deliver a printed message to every residential and business location in the nation. For this reason, the mail advertising and marketing community considers the preservation of a universal mail delivery system to be of vital importance.

The only universal mail delivery system that exists today is that which is maintained by the U.S. Postal Service. This stems primarily from the monopoly over the carriage of letter mail provided by Congress to the Postal Service. Congress also delegated to the Postal Service sole authority to define what constitutes letter mail.

As defined today, a letter consists of all matter that qualifies under postal rules as first class mail. Second class periodicals, such

The author is executive director of the Third Class Mail Association.

as newspapers and magazines, and fourth class mail matter, such as parcels, books, recordings, and films, are not covered by the letter mail monopoly. Unaddressed third class mail that is distributed on an area-wide saturation basis to every address also is not covered by the letter mail monopoly. But any third class mail matter that is distributed selectively or is addressed is considered letter mail. A piece of third class mail is considered addressed even when the scheme of distribution is listed on a separate piece of paper and not based on addresses actually affixed to the mail piece, or even when the scheme of distribution consists of memorized addresses within the mind of the deliverer. The Postal Service's treatment of catalogs represents yet another curious quirk in its definition of letter mail. Catalogs greater than 24 pages are not considered letters, but catalogs fewer than 24 pages are.

Primarily because the Postal Service's universal mail delivery represents for mail advertisers and marketers the only game in town, the advertising mail community's support for a universal mail system has evidenced itself as ardent support for the Postal Service, and, indeed, there historically has existed a symbiotic relationship between the Postal Service (and its predecessor institution, the Post Office Department) and the mail advertising community. But this long-time symbiotic relationship between the Postal Service and its third class mail customers has deteriorated in recent years because of chronically poor mail service, alarmingly high postal rate increases, and the prospects of even higher additional rate increases in the near future.

The growth of third class mail volume over the past several years has been phenomenal. Since 1980, third class mail volume has doubled. In postal FY 1987, the USPS delivered over 59 billion pieces of third class mail. Third class mail's proportionate share of USPS volume has been growing. In postal FY 1984, third class mail accounted for 34 percent of all mail carried by the Postal Service. Four years later, third class mail accounted for 38 percent of all mail volume.

This didn't happen quite by accident. In 1980, the Postal Service under the direction of then–postmaster general William F. Bolger, made a concerted effort to attract third class mail volume. The Postal Service's interest in cultivating new business was well received by advertisers interested in expanding their use of mail as a medium.

This invigorated relationship between the USPS and business promised to be a mutually beneficial one. The Postal Service would help mail marketers reach the audiences they desired, and mail marketers would provide the USPS with preprocessed, inexpensive-to-handle mail that would provide needed revenues to help defray the costs of running a universal mail delivery system.

Many within the advertising and marketing community, such as list brokers and managers, letter shops, printers, envelope manufacturers, computer service firms, advertising agencies, direct marketing consultants, and others, benefitted substantially from the subsequent third class mail growth. These companies, which form the infrastructure of the mail advertising and marketing industry, became reliant on third class mail's continued growth to ensure their own vitality. The Postal Service benefitted as well. Indeed, as recently as 1987, Deputy Postmaster General Michael S. Coughlin was telling audiences that "third class mail is the engine that's pulling the Postal Service's train." Without third class mail, the cost of a first class stamp would be higher.

In spite of this, a few years ago signs began to appear that growth of advertising mail volume was not all that welcome. In the early 1980s, industry-sponsored studies of USPS delivery service performance revealed that a significant amount of properly addressed, properly prepared third class mail was not getting delivered. In addition to the nondelivery problem, industry surveys, such as the mail-monitoring surveys sponsored by the Third Class Mail Association (TCMA), revealed that the USPS characteristically failed to meet its own standards for timely, albeit deferred, third class mail delivery.

These industry reports initially were greeted by postal officials with considerable skepticism, only to be followed by promises to set things straight. While third class mail service showed some slight improvement for a short period of time, subsequent industry studies and audits by postal inspectors revealed that service-related problems were as bad as ever. The twin problems of nondelivery and inconsistent and untimely delivery were costing mail marketers a fortune—not only in postage wasted on mail that was never delivered or was not delivered in a sufficiently timely manner to generate expected sales, but also in money wasted on printing, mail piece design, list rentals, other support services, and lost sales opportunities (undoubtedly the greatest loss of all).

Many postal veterans attribute third class mail's service-related problems to management's inability to anticipate mail volume growth and respond swiftly to meet accelerating demand. Postal worker productivity declined, as postal costs continued to rise. Management's inability to match personnel resources flexibly to workload needs exacerbated service-related problems, and the rigidity of union-imposed work rules limited management's array of alternatives. Overtime usage soared, and Bolger's successor, Paul N. Carlin, tried to remedy the service problems by going on a hiring spree. The size of the postal work force swelled, costs kept rising, and postal rate increases were imminent.

Evidence also began to emerge that the proportionate increase of advertising matter in the mail stream was alarming postal policy-makers. When the proposed 1984 rate increases were accepted by the governors, Postal Board Chairman John R. McKean expressed a great deal of concern over third class mail's growth and what he perceived as its disproportionate contribution to USPS revenues. McKean expressed an interest in using higher third class rates to control advertising mail volume growth. Discussions on using rates as a volume-controlling mechanism did not cease with McKean's departure from the board. In fact, such discussions occurred among postal managers immediately before the filing for the most recent postal rate increase.

While third class mail was experiencing a healthy rate of growth, first class mail's growth was snail-paced. Mail growth trends, especially business's burgeoning interest in alternative communications means (i.e., facsimile, electronic data interchange, electronic mail, electronic funds transfer, and telecommunications), suggested that third class mail's share of total mail volume soon would outstrip first class mail's proportionate share. The general public, it was suggested, might not look fondly on a postal service that predominantly carried advertising mail matter.

While a member of the Postal Board, former postal governor William F. Sullivan said that advertising mail volume should not be allowed to outstrip first class personal and business communications. A similar expression of concern was raised by Postal Rate Commissioner Patti Birge Tyson in advance of the 1987 postal rate case, and she echoed her concerns in a separate opinion filed with the commission's most recent postal rate recommendations. Specifically, Ms. Tyson said:

96

It is very important for the commission and the Postal Service to bear in mind the possibility of a time in the near future when [the volume of] third class mail delivered to private homes will exceed that of first class. While much of first class is sent to businesses in the form of bill payments and orders, most third class mail is targeted at the homeowner. The combination of an increasing share of the mail stream for third class and its targeting of individual postal customers means the average homeowner is finding his mailbox is a repository for unsolicited advertising messages rather than a source of business and personal communication.

This shift . . . to my mind it raises a serious concern about the American public's perception of the Postal Service and its mission. Both the commission and the Postal Service must face this issue in the process of developing future rate schedules.

In short, as far as mail marketers and advertisers were concerned, the handwriting was on the wall. Management is having a difficult time managing mail volume growth, and postal policymakers are questioning the propriety of the Postal Service's role relative to advertising mail.

The most recent postal rate increase for third class mailers—the largest in recent memory—was the last straw. The news that third class mail rates were to rise by more than 30 percent stunned the mail advertising and marketing community. But as large as the increases were, the Rate Commission made clear that it really had wanted to raise third class mail rates even higher. The only thing that held the commission back was the fear that higher rates would disrupt the Postal Service's ability to project accurately mail volumes and revenues, and truly would devastate business mailers.

Among the chief reasons for the alarming rate increases was that USPS costs were out of control. When the Postal Service first filed its rate case, it presented to the Rate Commission a wildly overstated revenue requirement request. The Postal Service, for instance, predicted that 40 percent of its eligible work force would elect to leave the Civil Service Retirement System (CSRS) and enroll in the new Federal Employees Retirement System (FERS), at a cost in excess of $1 billion. The actual FERS conversion rate turned out to be a meager 1.8 percent, amounting to a revenue-need overstatement of $894.2 million.

Everyone within the postal community expected the commission to trim rates across the board to reflect this revenue-need reduction. But between the May rate case filing date and the close of the public record in January, the Postal Service managed to run up sufficient expenses to wipe out the anticipated FERS savings. For instance, the service's collective bargaining agreement—the agreement that was so loudly proclaimed by postal management as a major accomplishment—cost the service some $291 million more than originally projected. (The actual figure, according to senior postal officials' most recent estimate, is closer to $500 million more than anticipated, and may be even higher.) The labor agreement's effect on non-bargaining-unit employee salaries boosted the revenue need an additional $67 million. Cost of living allowance increases added $32.7 million to the revenue need. Greater-than-anticipated employee health benefits costs added $191.1 million more. Increased COLA costs affected CSRS/FERS contributions and life insurance premium costs, and repriced annual leave costs and Postal Service civil service retirement unfunded liabilities boosted the revenue need as well.

The failure of former postmaster general Preston R. Tisch's much-touted FY 1987 cost-containment program made matters worse. Tisch had asked postal managers to trim $363 million from the operating budget. The service was able to trim only $149 million from its expense base—a shortfall of $214 million. As a result, although the service had projected an FY 1987 loss of $115 million, it realized a loss of $223 million. The sad note to all this is that postal managers, at least according to the testimony of one of the Postal Service's rate case witnesses, had "not undertaken any new initiatives with respect to its cost containment program, and . . . [proceeded in the case] on the assumption that its level of attainment" of any savings would not improve between the time of the rate case and the beginning of the FY 1989 test year.

The Postal Service compounded the bad news by opposing mailer efforts to mitigate the effects of the new rates through new cost-saving, work-sharing incentive programs. For instance, when it originally filed its case, the Postal Service recommended the creation of new work-sharing discounts for second class mailers who prepare their mail on pallets instead of in sacks, but opposed a similar program for third class mail—even though the savings and efficiencies from a third class pallet program would be as great as, or greater than, from a second class program. TCMA strongly recommended the creation of a third class mail postal-rate-discount program for palletized mail, in spite of strong Postal Service objections. While the commission recommended a new classification category for palletized third class mail, it backed away from recommending a rate discount.

A consortium of third class mailers recommended the adoption of drop-shipment discounts for mail that is transported privately and entered at destination bulk mail centers, sectional center facilities, and associate offices. The Postal Service vigorously opposed the proposal on the grounds that the operational and financial impacts of a drop-shipment program were unknown, and could adversely affect postal operations and finances. The commission yielded to the service's arguments, and the drop-shipment idea was lost.

The Postal Service also opposed a petition from another consortium of third class mailers for the creation of a new subclass for carrier-route presorted mail. The commission again sided with the service, and that proposal was lost.

The only light of hope, albeit a dim one, came from a TCMA-backed recommendation for a new work-sharing/discount program for letter-size, automatable bulk third class mail carrying ZIP + 4 codes and/or nine-digit bar codes. While the Postal Service originally had not proposed such a program, it eventually supported the idea, and the commission recommended adoption, but with lower discounts than TCMA had advocated.

In short, the Postal Service's opposition to several mailer-backed work-sharing/discount and mail classification proposals thwarted efforts to reward mailers for the cost-saving work they performed.

Current law requires postal rates to be cost-based. As USPS costs rises, rates must rise. Today, 85 percent of all postal costs are labor-related, and those costs are rising. With nothing on the horizon to suggest these costs will be lessened, the prospect of even larger third class mail rate increases is alarming mailers. The mail advertising and marketing industry is volume driven. It needs an unconstrained ability to grow, and the current postal cost-rate spiral is threatening to constrain the industry's growth.

Judging from postal management's inability to contain labor costs over the collective-bargaining table, from its apparent unwillingness to use contracting out as a way of lessening labor costs, and from its unwillingness to explore *expeditiously* the cost-saving benefits of mailer work sharing, third class mailers are left with only one option—to free themselves from the constraints over the carriage and delivery of addressed third class mail and explore the viability of lowering mail-related costs by using private delivery alternatives.

In January 1988 the TCMA testified before the President's Commission on Privatization and called for an end to the letter mail prohibition on the carriage and delivery of addressed third class mail. TCMA emphasized that it was *not* calling for a wholesale abolition of the private express statutes. For an industry whose economic vitality is inextricably interwoven with the need for an economical, universal mail delivery system, doing otherwise would have been reckless and foolhardy. Abolishing the private express statutes in their entirety without knowing whether private, competitive mail delivery would ensure the maintenance of a universal delivery network would be venturing into areas where angels, let alone public officials, fear to tread. Nor was the association saying the USPS should be prohibited from carrying addressed third class mail. It simply said the Postal Service should not be the only entity entitled to delivery third class mail.

On March 16, 1988, prompted by concerns over escalating postal costs and rates and substandard third class service, TCMA petitioned Postmaster General Anthony M. Frank to initiate immediately a rule-making proceeding for the suspension of the private express statutes as they presently apply to addressed third class mail. Ample precedents for suspension of the statutes already exist, urgent letters, international remailing, and newspapers and magazines, for example. In essence, mail advertisers and marketers are ready to face the risks associated with permitting private delivery of addressed third class mail.

Allowing the private carriage and delivery of addressed third class mail should provide a stimulus for the development of alternative private-sector services. Some private delivery systems already exist, but their development has been hampered substantially by the limited kind of mail matter the law permits them to carry. Suspension of the private express statutes for addressed third class mail would make an additional 59 billion pieces of mail available to private enterprise. This amount should spur the development of private-sector delivery firms that eventually could compete head-to-head with the Postal Service in carrying and delivering nationally distributed addressed bulk third class mail.

The inevitable competition among private delivery companies, and between private-sector firms and the Postal Service, should benefit the users of all mail services. Competition would not be limited to price alone. To have lasting appeal to direct mail advertisers, private deliverers would have to provide services at least comparable, but preferably superior, to the Postal Service's, such as offering targeted guaranteed days of delivery or finding superior methods for handling the problems associated with mail delivery in multioccupant business and residential buildings. To maintain its share of the advertising mail market, the Postal Service would have to contain its rates to make its prices competitive, and it would have to improve the timeliness and consistency of its delivery service.

Permitting the private carriage of addressed third class mail can provide an excellent means for assessing the value of private, competitive mail delivery. If private delivery proves to be a success, then our nation's policymakers will better know the benefits that can be derived from private-sector alternatives. In a very real sense, third class mail can serve as the nation's laboratory for testing the private delivery concept. Without such a test, wholesale abandonment of the private express statutes would put the nation needlessly at risk by destroying the only universal mail delivery system that currently exists. It's time to put the concept to an effective test.

10. The Need for Alternatives to the Postal Monopoly

Richard A. Barton

As an official of the Direct Marketing Association and representative of its three thousand corporate members, I will address primarily the concerns of third class mailers. However, members of the association have a deep involvement in all classes of mail and, therefore, have a very strong interest in a viable national delivery system. In the past, this interest has centered almost exclusively on the United States Postal Service, and we have been strong supporters of it. We still are.

However, recent events have caused our members to reevaluate. Even the sacred cows, most particularly the private express statutes, are sacred no longer. While we have not yet taken a position on repeal or modification of these statutes which cover the nation's postal monopoly, DMA's board believes that they, too, must undergo intense reexamination.

The "recent events" to which I am referring are the growing evidence of serious delivery problems and the recent debilitating postal rate increase visited upon third class mailers.

We have been working with the Postal Service on delivery problems ever since the DMA/Doubleday study in 1981 showed that unacceptable amounts of properly addressed third class mail simply were not being delivered. To be completely fair, postal management for several years has been hard at work on a problem which even they admit exists. However, a growing number of further studies by DMA, other associations, individual companies, and the Postal Service itself have consistently revealed the persistence of the problem.

Nondelivery is not a problem merely because of wasted postage, paper, and printing costs. It costs companies even more through

The author is senior vice president of the Direct Marketing Association.

the loss of sales and customers. Many companies put the estimated losses in the millions of dollars. Add to this the documented evidence of slow and inconsistent delivery, sale notices which arrive after the sale, and some damaged mail, and there is little doubt that there is a significant level of waste and inefficiency in the delivery system. Some of this is inevitable in any delivery system. However, many DMA members who are responsible for mailing billions of pieces have reached the conclusion that the current postal delivery system is doing them economic harm.

The recent postal rate increase is the second element of this postal double whammy. The Postal Service cited an average third class increase of 25 percent. However, technical rules changes that apply to third class mailers spell far higher increases for a substantial number of major mailers. Also, because of an even higher increase for the basic bulk rate, many smaller mailers will be hurt or, worse, simply go out of business.

The amount of the increase is not nearly as disturbing as the reasons for it and the implications which the actions of the Postal Rate Commission and the USPS Board of Governors have for the future. First, there are many indications, some of them contained within the written opinion of the Postal Rate Commission, that subjective judgments played an important role. We keep hearing statements from postal and commission officials about the "image" of third class mail and concern that third class volume may exceed first class volume in the near future. These statements may or may not be true, but they should not, indeed *may* not, form the principal foundation of postal rate decisions under the Postal Reorganization Act of 1970. Some subjective judgments are allowed under the act. However, we have the disturbing feeling that these subjective judgments were the driving force behind the increased attribution of costs in certain areas. There is every indication that these attitudes will cause third class rates to soar even higher in the next rate case.

Two other factors in the last rate case give us cause for great concern. The first is that neither the Postal Service nor the Postal Rate Commission gives more than lip service to established economic models for efficient pricing of products or services. On top of that, the commission virtually abdicated all responsibility for keeping some check on escalating postal costs. It accepted all of

104

the Postal Service's requests for revenue, including a midstream adjustment when it became evident that the Postal Service had misjudged the cost of its employees converting to the new Federal Employees Retirement System by almost a billion dollars. Finally, the Board of Governors added insult to injury by implementing the increase *three months* before the implementation date upon which the revenue requirement was based, and at least *two weeks* before postal management had suggested that mailers and postal employees alike prepare for implementation. Little wonder that mailers using all classes of mail believe they are looking at a system which is uncontrolled and, perhaps, uncontrollable.

We believe that the mailing community must examine every alternative to the Postal Service for delivery of its advertising messages and its products. As our president, Jonah Gitlitz, has said:

> The only social and economic justification for a sanctioned monopoly in the United States is that it operate efficiently and at reasonable cost to its users—consumers and business alike. That is the challenge to the USPS today. If it loses that justification, then we must be given the freedom to utilize alternative means.

No mailer can afford to be subjected to a delivery system that fails to deliver its product in a timely and consistent way, is subject to little in the way of cost control, and to a significant extent is subject neither to competitive pressures nor to a pricing model which substitutes for those competitive factors.

For these reasons, we believe it is important for the economic health of direct marketing to search for viable alternatives.

11. How to Privatize the Postal Service

Stuart M. Butler

Introduction

The case for some degree of privatization of postal services is overwhelming. As others have pointed out, the U.S. Postal Service suffers from the classic attributes of a monopoly with its hands in the taxpayers' till.

Not surprisingly, the pattern of its behavior has been quite similar to that of Europe's nationalized industries. The USPS, like Europe's state-run firms, maintains the fiction that it is a public service, and yet it is run in the interest of its employees, with the customer receiving the worst level of service the monopoly can get away with. Any attempt to restrain bloated budgets and giveaways to employees elicits cutbacks in service designed to provoke angry public demands on Congress to reinstate funds—Europeans know this process very well. And while USPS managers and unions put efficiency and the public last, they are paragons of efficiency when it comes to protecting their gravy train, devoting enormous amounts of time, money, and manpower to courting key congressional committees and coopting or simply threatening members of Congress. If a lawmaker wants to see letters move through the USPS system at remarkable speed, he need only make a speech mildly criticizing the Postal Service—he will be inundated with letters from angry and aggrieved mail carriers, delivered with admirable promptness.

Only instituting a measure of competition, which in practice means some degree of privatization, will provide both business and ordinary Americans with the quality and efficiency they have every right to expect. Yet there is a big difference between recognizing privatization as a worthy goal and developing a strategy to bring it

The author is director of domestic policy at the Heritage Foundation.

about. Viewing the problem as a matter of business organization, we could devise a number of models that would transform the mail delivery system into an efficient, competitive privatized service. But while any privatization model must pass such a "business plan" test of economic soundness, it must also pass a test of political practicability.

Privatization, like nationalization, is first and foremost a political exercise. It requires strategists to deal with powerful political forces and interest groups, and to advance proposals that create favorable dynamics. This is no easy undertaking. Nevertheless, the lessons of both failed and successful privatization campaigns, especially in such countries as Britain, where major state-owned monopolies have been privatized, are reason for some optimism in the case of the Postal Service.

Elsewhere, I and my colleagues at the Heritage Foundation have developed privatization models for the USPS.[1] These models explore variants of a few central themes. In particular, they focus on employee ownership, a "buy out" approach to current employees, contracting out and the sale of franchises, and a system of privatization that maintains the current structure of uniform pricing, a unified system, and the core of the private express statutes. Rather than go into the details of these plans, elements of which appear in models proposed by many advocates of privatization, I will discuss the political dynamics of the USPS which have led us at Heritage to believe that a successful privatization strategy must contain certain key features.

The Political Constraints

Most Americans have a love-hate relationship with the Postal Service, usually with hate edging out love. Customers tend to have some genuine affection for their mail carrier, at the same time as they rail against misdirected and delayed letters, lines at the post office, and the ever-climbing cost of a stamp. The political process, however, is incapable of translating this almost universal public grumbling into structural reform.

[1]See Stuart M. Butler, *Privatizing Federal Spending* (New York: Universe Books, 1985), chap. 5; Butler, "Privatizing Bulk Mail," *Management* 6, no. 1, 1986; Stephen Moore, "Privatizing the U.S. Postal Service," in Moore and Butler, *Privatization* (Washington: Heritage Foundation, 1987), chap. 2.

One reason for this is that precisely because USPS employees gain so many benefits from the monopoly, they have powerful incentives to lobby Congress to protect their status. Thus congressional committees come under enormous pressure from the postal unions. So, even though individual lawmakers recognize the public's irritation with the USPS, well-financed and aggressive union lobbying invariably wins the day.

The other principal reason for the success of USPS unions in defusing public anger is what one might call the devil-you-know effect. While ordinary Americans complain bitterly about the quality and cost of the service, the Postal Service is at least a known quantity. Many fear that if the private express statutes were to be repealed, on the other hand, and free competition were to follow, the result would produce both winners and losers among customers. And while there would be significant economic gains overall, and although advocates for privatization can identify beneficiaries, there is sufficient uncertainty about the outcome that average Americans hesitate to jump into the unknown of full deregulation.

Postal Service union leaders, as one might expect, are expert in appealing to these doubts. Consider a recent letter to the *Wall Street Journal* by Vincent Sombrotto, president of the National Association of Letter Carriers:

> Privatization would create a fragmented, confusing postal system subject to disruptions from bankruptcies, unregulated mergers, and the general instability of private competition. The declining quality of mail services following privatization would make the service deterioration observed in the wake of airline deregulation look mild in comparison. And mailers, particularly those who live in rural and inner-city areas, probably would pay more for postal services as firms seek to establish local monopolies and charge whatever the market would bear.[2]

It is hard to imagine more illogicalities, innuendoes, and falsehoods being packed into one paragraph. Nevertheless, such claims do not have to be true. They need only appear plausible to the nonexpert to undermine public support for structural reform.

[2]Letter to the editor, *Wall Street Journal*, April 5, 1988.

Guidelines for a Privatization Strategy

To stand any chance of success, a model for privatization must address this political environment. In particular, it must do three things: identify and mobilize a constituency that will gain directly from privatization, and thereby create a force that will have an interest in sustaining a campaign; assure the general public that it can only gain from privatization, thereby undercutting devil-you-know resistance to change; and compensate USPS employees for potential losses—or better still, provide them with a vested interest in supporting privatization. If a proposal does not incorporate each of these components, gaining congressional support is likely to prove impossible.

A Pro-Privatization Constituency

Most privatization proposals achieve the first requirement of generating a constituency in favor of the change. Selling the USPS by a discounted stock sale, like the British Telecom privatization in 1984, would lead to a large number of immediate gainers who could be expected to support the move. But the gainers would be politically diffuse and unlikely to be a major lobbying influence in the early, crucial stage of the debate. Moreover, a proposal involving the creation of an efficient new corporation might well encounter opposition from private firms whose business prospers thanks to USPS inefficiency.

Models that rely on deregulation, such as a straightforward repeal of the private express statutes, or on contracting out to large firms already in the communications field, would provide benefits to a more defined and better-organized constituency. This would mean more potent pro-privatization lobbying at the critical early stages. On the other hand, there is always the danger that rivalry between potential contract bidders or buyers, or among potential new entrants in a regime of deregulation, could blunt such lobbying. When the Department of Transportation was urging the sale of Conrail to Norfolk Southern as its preferred bidder, for instance, it encountered resistance from disappointed rival suitors. Ultimately, the successful strategy was a proposal for a public offering.

Reducing Public Anxiety

Fear among the public that there will be substantial losers under a privatization proposal could prove fatal to the plan. Proponents

110

of any proposal leaving the door open to a counterattack by USPS unions will immediately be thrown on the defensive and have little chance of ultimate success. Ideally there must be near-universal public support for privatization if the campaign is to win congressional backing. But at the very least, there must be no clear losers or general public anxiety about the outcome.

For this reason any proposal hinging on repeal of the private express statutes would seem to be a political nonstarter. A powerful economic and equity case can be made for repeal, of course, but the political case is very weak. Chipping away at the edges of the monopoly makes good sense: small erosions here and there do not normally evoke widespread concern based on uncertainty, and each modest victory leads to greater public acceptability and thus provides a foundation for the next push. But a frontal attack on the statutes would be political suicide. The postal unions would have a field day with charges of the Sombrotto variety. While these could be dealt with, trying to rebut them would draw privatization proponents deeper and deeper into a quagmire of technicalities and economic analysis, leaving the public confused and increasingly skeptical.

The alternative is to maintain the principles of uniform pricing and a universal system, but introduce free competition under contract for the supply of services to that system. In this way the public could be given two firm guarantees. First, no group of customers would face a differential price by virtue of location. Thus, union arguments to the effect that a senior citizen in rural Iowa would face huge price hikes under open competition could be brushed aside. And second, all customers would only gain from privatization, since competition could only reduce the cost of providing elements of the overall system, with the savings distributed through uniform pricing. By making this tactical concession, privatization then becomes a no-lose prospect for all Americans.

Many possible models would fit such an approach. Systematic contracting out of loss-making Postal Service functions, and the sale of temporary franchise rights for profitable functions, for instance, would introduce private-sector competition throughout the system and a downward pressure on costs and prices. Profits from franchises might be used as a pool of funds to subsidize contractors for loss-making delivery routes and other unprofitable functions.

Employee-owned enterprises, designed to elicit postal employee support for privatization, could be incorporated into such a framework, just as they could into complete deregulation.

Needless to say, an approach that rejects complete deregulation is unattractive in many respects. It reduces the degree of potential competition and innovation, and hence does not produce the highest possible efficiency benefits for the customer. It maintains unfair cross-subsidies that reduce overall economic efficiency. It presents greater opportunities for government meddling through regulation. But it has one distinct virtue: It has a chance of success in Congress. Repeal of the private express statutes currently does not.

Gaining Support among USPS Employees

The USPS work force constitutes the biggest roadblock facing privatization. With wages and benefits well above market rates, thanks to monopoly rents and management "negotiators" who have little incentive to resist pay demands, postal workers and their union representatives understandably see privatization as a threat. And they have demonstrated time and time again that in a head-to-head political confrontation they are almost impossible to beat.

That political reality suggests strongly that privatization strategists should concentrate on proposals designed to compensate workers for potential losses from privatization and to reward workers who support privatization. To accomplish this, proponents of a private USPS would be well-advised to look carefully at the experience of Britain.

Margaret Thatcher faced a daunting prospect as her Conservative government launched its privatization drive in the early 1980s. Heavily unionized public-sector monopolies dominated the country's utilities, exerting enormous political pressure by taking strike action against the public whenever union interests were threatened. Even government-appointed managers tended to "go native" and resist change. Yet the privatization of vast areas of the government's holdings, including the entire telephone system, was achieved smoothly.

Thatcher's commanding parliamentary majority meant that she could have pushed through privatization legislation even in the teeth of entrenched opposition, although previous experience suggested that with determined worker opposition the legislation might well have been unworkable. But in practice, there was virtually no significant employee opposition to privatization. On the contrary, in many instances the employees vigorously embraced the policy. In the sale of British Telecom, the telephone system, for instance, some 96 percent of workers defied union instructions and actually bought stock in the privatized company. Employees of British Airways complained bitterly when at one point the timetable for privatization was delayed. And employees of the National Freight Corporation, a huge trucking firm, actually bought the government-owned firm outright. No doubt, the idea that USPS workers could ever accept, let alone support, privatization seems inconceivable, but it was equally inconceivable that public-sector workers in Britain would accommodate to the policy. The reasons the British workers did so could provide some important lessons for Postal Service privatization in this country.

The key to Thatcher's success was a conscious strategy of "buying out" the implicit job and pension property rights of public-sector workers. Conservative officials recognized that the efficiency benefits associated with private ownership would be enhanced if workers generally supported the change. Thus, work force acceptance would increase the value of a firm to potential buyers, and hence the price they would pay. For this reason, it made good business sense to provide compensation and inducements to workers to accept the change, since that "investment" would be recaptured in the market price for the asset or in net economic benefits to the nation.

Several devices were adopted. Before actual privatization, workers were offered generous redundancy payments if they were willing to quit. Despite the size of many of these payments, usually they were considerably lower than the present value of each worker's likely future earnings and benefits. Workers accepted the payments because they placed a greater value on immediate cash, and because they were free to take a new job. And because of chronic overmanning in most nationalized firms (like the USPS), providing such payments made economic sense even though the firm lost the services of the employee, since streamlining the work force actually improved total productivity.

Having increased the value of the firm and improved the climate for privatization by such tactics, the government took further steps

113

to win over employees in its specific proposals for sales. Although details differed in each case, the general approach was to provide employees with a free ownership stake in the new firm, which could be turned into immediate cash or held for future income and profit. This ranged from some free stock and a discount price for additional purchases in the case of British Telecom, to outright employee ownership at a cut-rate price in the case of National Freight. In addition, the managers of most companies, judged by government officials to be key to the political and business success of privatization, were awarded very generous stock options and other inducements to win their support.

Even with its ability to push through privatization legislation, the Thatcher government believed that these inducements made good political—and economic—sense. In the United States, with its more decentralized political power centers, buy-out strategies are essential if the political dynamics are ever to shift decisively in favor of privatization.

With the Postal Service, a range of employee inducements would be possible. The system's vast real estate holdings are an extremely valuable asset and could be used as security to provide redundancy payments and other inducements. Given the potential future budget savings available from privatization, even a direct appropriation to liquidate pension liabilities and other future costs could make good sense, since streamlining labor costs would enhance the cash value of the system.

Other labor protections and inducements could also serve to reduce employee fears and opposition. In a contracting-out model of privatization, for instance, labor protections used by many cities could be adopted, such as no-layoff agreements and requirements on contractors to hire public-sector employees. Although such protections reduce the benefits of contracting out (but not by as much as one might think, since many of the savings come from managerial innovation), they can accelerate the process by addressing union concerns.

Ownership inducements could also prove effective in reducing employee opposition to privatization. Why would postal workers now enjoying enormous benefits as employees ever want to take the risk of becoming owners under a more competitive framework? It depends on the terms. For instance, if workers in the bulk mail

114

systems were given the opportunity to take ownership of the capital assets of the system, and given the right to compete more aggressively with UPS, such as by entering into agreements with convenience stores for pickup services, the potential for profit might well encourage many workers to give serious consideration to privatization.

Such employee-ownership ideas concentrate benefits linked to privatization on a group that currently provides the momentum against privatization. In contrast to privatization models that simply throw the system open to competition, or that sell USPS assets to the highest bidder or to the general public, some degree of employee ownership would create a vested interest among workers in favor of privatization. In Britain, these ownership devices were critical in achieving at least the acquiescence of labor. They were also effective in detaching ordinary workers, who tend to be most interested in shorter-term financial benefits, from their more ideological union leaders, who often oppose privatization on principle. In the United States, with its long tradition of blue-collar share ownership, the tactic might be even more successful—even among postal workers. Ownership inducements thus should be a key feature of any plan to privatize the Postal Service.

The Postal Service clearly is not an easy target for privatization. It is an integral part of American life. Most Americans depend on it, with all its deficiencies, for routine communication, and are not inclined to embrace radical privatization. And it has some of the most powerful unions in the country—unions highly adept in public relations and hardball lobbying. To have any chance of success, a strategy to privatize the system will have to be far more than an elegant business plan that makes good commercial sense. It will have to be a political battle plan designed both to appeal to the powerful interest groups, which influence the legislative process, and to calm the fears of a general public easily dissuaded from plunging into the unknown.

12. Privatizing the Postal Service: Why Do It; How to Do It

Bert Ely

Introduction

Privatizing the United States Postal Service (USPS) is and always has been a very viable proposition because any postal service is a relatively simple, straightforward business activity: revenues are collected from individual users of the service in exchange for the provision of specific postal services to those users. There is no unique welfare element inherent in a postal service that precludes its privatization. While a postal service provides what some may consider to be an essential service, other distributors of essential services, such as water, telephone, natural gas, and electric utilities, function very well as privately owned entities.

The entire USPS—not just a portion of it—should be privatized through a carefully structured sale of the entire operation to private owners. This chapter first discusses why this approach is the most desirable. It then discusses how a privatized postal service could become a solid moneymaker as the ability to operate profitably is essential to any privatization. Next, the chapter outlines how the privatization transaction should be financed. It then describes the likely sources of opposition to privatization and suggests sources of support for it. The chapter closes by summarizing major issues any postal privatization proposal must address.

Reasons to Privatize the Entire USPS

Proposals to privatize just some portions of the USPS, such as delivery routes or retail branches, are not feasible for operational, political, and other strategic reasons. Piecemeal privatization, which is simply contracting out by a government-owned entity,

The author is president of Ely & Company, a financial institutions consulting firm in Alexandria, Virginia.

would do nothing more than cannibalize USPS and most likely further worsen its service. Thus, serious consideration should be given only to proposals to privatize the entire USPS.

Privatization of just parts of a postal operation is not feasible for operational reasons because the entire postal activity, from mail collection to delivery, is very sensitive to even momentary delays. The existing privatization of a crucial part of postal operations— the intercity hauling of mail—already accounts for much of the unreliability of first class (letter) mail delivery. Airline deregulation has caused USPS tremendous scheduling problems in recent years, particularly in reducing the percentage of first class mail scheduled for second and third day delivery, yet USPS is barred from operating its own airplanes to haul first class mail. The vested interest that contract truckers have in hauling intercity mail has also bred additional inflexibility into postal operations. Like any other interest group, these truckers use the political process to protect this interest.

The operations of Federal Express and United Parcel Service reinforce this point. They contract out very few of their operating activities. Each operates its own fleet of planes, long-haul trucks, stations, and delivery vehicles. As Federal Express grew, it steadily reduced its dependence on outside air hauling and ground delivery services. A postal service experiences the same hour-to-hour and sometimes minute-to-minute need to tightly control its delivery cycle. Therefore, substantial contracting out of postal operations is not desirable operationally.

In addition, piecemeal privatization is not feasible for political reasons. Attempting to contract out additional pieces of USPS will throw each piece into the political arena, since each newly contracted activity would quickly become a vested political interest. The postal unions, of course, almost certainly will oppose all contracting proposals, as high-wage unions invariably do. For example, a postal union recently was successful in opposing an effort by USPS to have Sears employees operate postal outlets in some Sears stores.

Existing private interests also will fight the contracting out of certain postal activities. For example, office supply stores might again oppose the contracting out of postal retail operations (the window counter operations in the post offices) because they would fear that retail contractors would attempt to sell mailing supplies.

118

Several years ago, the office-supply-store industry successfully blocked USPS from selling even a very limited line of such supplies in post offices. United Parcel Service might oppose any attempt to contract mail delivery, since the delivery contractors also might attempt to deliver small packages in competition with UPS.

Piecemeal privatization also would bar the effective use of ownership incentives for postal employees, specifically, broad-based employee stock ownership. Such ownership will be necessary to swing the support of USPS employees towards privatization. Moreover, an Employee Stock Ownership Plan (ESOP) would be feasible only if USPS itself is privatized. This use of an ESOP will be discussed below.

Contracting out portions of a postal operation may in fact be justifiable. However, each contracting decision, which is nothing more than a make-versus-buy decision, can more rationally be made once USPS has been privatized. First privatize the government enterprise and then start contracting out certain functions, rather than first contracting out pieces of the government enterprise before privatizing what is left.

Privatizing the entire USPS best lends itself to the rationale for privatizing any government activity—make it better, not just more efficient. The postal service can provide better *and* more efficient service only if USPS is privatized in its entirety.

Making a Private Postal Service Profitable

Although USPS has suffered modest losses in recent years, a privatized postal service could easily become a solid moneymaker by reducing costs and building the volume of its business. In fact, achieving sufficient profitability to earn an adequate return on its equity capital is essential to achieving a viable privatization of USPS. As will be explained below, a privatized postal service would have to earn a pretax profit of at least 4.2 percent of its revenues to attract sufficient capital to finance its privatization.

During USPS's FY 1988 (October 1, 1987, to September 30, 1988), the operating activities of USPS other than actual mail delivery accounted for 71 percent of all USPS expenses. These nondelivery activities offer substantial cost-cutting opportunities. Many cost-cutting innovations also would improve postal service and thus increase the volume of business.

One measure to cut costs would involve rerouting a substantial portion of intercity first class mail through one national air hub to provide one- to two-day mail service in the continental United States. This, of course, is how Federal Express operates. UPS also uses an air hub in Nashville for its next-day air service and much of its second-day service. A postal service air hub most probably would be located at the Memphis, Nashville, or St. Louis airports, or possibly at its own airport in that region. This hub would reship bulk lots (bundles, bags, containers, etc.) of mail moving between the 479 postal sectional centers. There would be no sorting of individual letters at the hub; all letter sorting would be confined to the sending and receiving sectional centers. Use of one hub would substantially reduce overall postal costs by minimizing mail handling and rehandling expenses.

Where volume warranted, however, mail might move directly by truck or rail rather than through the national air hub. Federal Express now bypasses its Memphis hub for some parcels, particularly for those moving in the East out of New York. Thus, mail moving between two cities would not pass through the hub if direct air or ground haulage between them could be justified.

On the basis of preliminary studies, it appears that two-day first class mail service could be provided between almost any two points within the continental United States for no more than what it now costs to move intercity mail, and possibly for less. The balance of all letter mail, including mail to and from Hawaii, Alaska, and Puerto Rico, could be delivered in three days. With a national air hub, it should be feasible to match the 98 percent delivery reliability Federal Express strives for. By contrast, USPS claims that in 1988 it achieved 86 percent reliability for mail scheduled for two-day delivery (within a 600-mile radius of its mailing point) and 89 percent reliability for mail scheduled for three-day delivery (cross-country delivery).

A national air hub would not be a factor in providing overnight delivery for local mail. Trucks or possibly a special rail service would handle this cartage.

Gearing a national air hub to a two-day delivery cycle should enable a postal service to achieve a much higher aircraft utilization than Federal Express achieves. In particular, air cartage of non–first class mail during off-peak hours would greatly increase aircraft utilization. Thus, a postal service operating its own air hub, and its own airplanes, should be able to move intercity mail for a lower total cost per pound than Federal Express can or than USPS probably now achieves through its existing network of contract air and truck services.

A national air hub, particularly if it were at an airport used exclusively by the Postal Service, would quickly be surrounded by national distribution and fulfillment centers that could use both the incoming and outgoing mail capabilities of the hub to rapidly process and fill mail orders. Federal Express's "PartsBank" offers this type of fulfillment capability, but on a limited scale. Such facilities would generate much captive volume for the postal service.

A second measure to reduce costs would be dropping the nine-digit ZIP Code in favor of a unique number for every mail delivery point. The nine-digit ZIP Code was ill-conceived because it does not permit the eventual full automation of the mail-sequencing process. Full automation requires that each mail delivery point (a home, business, or post office box) have its own unique, unduplicated number. Thus, the nine-digit ZIP Code should be replaced with a 10- or 11-digit "Mailing Code" (the existing five-digit ZIP Code plus another five or six digits). Each of the country's 115 million mail delivery points could then be assigned a unique Mailing Code. The Mailing Code would be much like a telephone number, in that any piece of mail would reach its destination if just that number appeared on the envelope or parcel.

The Mailing Code number should be structured so that one digit serves as a "check digit." Check digits, which are widely used where data accuracy is essential, enable computers to catch most errors in recording a number, whether the recording error is a simple transposition or a more complicated jumbling of digits. A Mailing Code with a check digit would greatly aid mass mailers, for example, in detecting addressing errors when entering subscriptions and orders and opening new accounts, or before mailing bills or packages. Likewise, the private postal service could use the check digit feature to catch incorrectly written Mailing Codes at a letter's entry point into the postal system. Catching and promptly correcting these errors would substantially reduce misdeliveries and greatly increase Postal Service reliability.

Eventually, as the necessary machinery is developed, the private postal service could use the Mailing Code to automatically sequence mail for mail carriers. USPS estimated that in FY 1988 letter carriers spent almost one-half of their workday sequencing the mail they would then deliver. This sequencing activity cost $3.5 billion in 1988 and accounted for almost 10 percent of USPS's total expenses. Automated sequencing would allow carriers to spend more of their workday actually delivering the mail. This productivity improvement would reduce mail-handling costs and probably broaden the areas where overnight mail delivery could be offered.

A third cost-reduction measure would entail radically restructuring and trimming parcel post. USPS's parcel post operation, which very feebly competes against United Parcel Service, almost certainly loses money. To some extent, parcel post operates independently of USPS's main postal service. Specifically, parcel post has separate regional bulk mail centers, where parcels are sorted along with other bulk mail shipments. Larger parcels also are delivered through a separate delivery system. Thus, discontinuing parcel post is feasible from an operations perspective. However, it might be possible to salvage some aspects of USPS's parcel post operation, in particular the very extensive network of post offices where parcels can be mailed. One possibility, which would have to be negotiated with UPS, would be for the private postal service to discontinue its separate delivery system. Instead, the parcels it collected would be fed into United Parcel's distribution and delivery system, particularly larger and heavier parcels that the postal service's letter carriers cannot easily deliver.

A final way to reduce costs is to increase productivity. To do this the privatized postal service should make greater use of part-time employees, revise its pay structure, and invest substantially in equipment. Some of these improvements would have to be negotiated with the postal work force; however, the opportunity for employees to participate in the ownership of a private postal service should help to pave the way for increased productivity.

Part-time employees should be used to a much greater extent for mail sorting and retail operations. Federal Express and UPS make heavy use of part-timers in their sorting operations; there is no reason why a private postal service could not do the same. Part-timers also should be used to meet peak-load requirements at post office retail windows, much as banks increasingly use part-time employees to meet their peak-time needs for tellers. This would enable a private postal service to more efficiently provide evening and weekend retail services at far more post offices than now offer such service.

Part-timers also could be used to make deliveries, specifically to make business deliveries and to put up mail addressed to post office boxes by 9:00 a.m. Beginning-of-the-day business delivery service would cut into Federal Express and local delivery services and undoubtedly boost business-to-business mail volume that facsimile machines increasingly transmit.

USPS employee turnover is sufficiently high that substantial use of part-time employees could be implemented within a few years after privatizing USPS.

The postal union labor contracts undoubtedly have excessive job classifications and make-work job rules. Tough negotiation and a buy-out of existing work rules through the privatization process would enable the management of a private postal service to utilize its employees more flexibly, and thus more productively. These negotiations also should strive for lower shift differentials so as to lessen the management bias against evening and night work. This bias has greatly slowed mail delivery in recent years.

Under private ownership, management could end USPS's tremendous pay structure compression under which supervisors earn little more, and sometimes less, than their subordinates. As of September 30, 1988, the postmaster general, who is the chief executive of USPS, earned $99,500 annually, while the average annual base pay of unionized postal employees in FY 1988 was $26,400. By being able to pay higher salaries, a private postal service would be able to improve the caliber of its supervision and operations management and thus improve overall postal service productivity.

Substantial capital investments in equipment also should be made to improve productivity. The USPS has been woefully deficient in investing in equipment. Instead, like governments generally, USPS has invested far more heavily in buildings and land. From September 30, 1985, to September 30, 1988, USPS increased its investment in real estate by $2.4 billion, or 50 percent. Over the same three-year period, it increased its investment in equipment by $1.1 billion, or 36 percent. The need to correct USPS's misallocation of its capital investments can be seen from another perspective: On September 30, 1988, 64 percent of USPS's investment was in real estate and 36 percent in equipment. At Federal Express and UPS, about 90 percent of their investment is in equipment.

Sectional centers, where incoming and outgoing mail is sorted, would especially benefit from greater capital investment, specifically in equipment that will work with greater reliability than some of USPS's recent automation investments. This is an aspect of postal operations where better management would earn substantial returns. Also, only 24,000 postal window clerks are presently equipped with "integrated retail terminals," in effect cash registers tailored to post office window operations. There is no reason why most, if not all, of the 100,000 or more post office windows should not be so equipped.

Private owners would move faster to cut costs and improve productivity through equipment investments. Apart from the profit incentive, managers in a private postal service would have much greater flexibility and more capital investment funds to use in reducing operating costs. Also, a private postal service would escape the periodic government-wide budget cuts that force sudden, drastic curtailments in capital outlays. That type of event happened during 1988, with the result that USPS had to trim its 1988 capital outlays by 74 percent.

In conjunction with reducing costs, a profitable private postal service will strive to increase the volume of its business. No matter how efficient a private postal service might become, it still will possess a large, fixed-cost delivery system. But the incremental cost of delivering additional pieces of mail should be relatively low if they are not bulky or especially heavy. Increasing physical volume consequently has a tremendous potential to increase the profitability of a postal service. Two measures—improving delivery service and adopting aggressive marketing strategies—are key to increasing the volume of business.

To improve service the postal system should increase the speed and reliability of delivery. While delivery slowness hurts mail volume, a far greater problem is the unpredictability of mail arrival. This is true for advertising mail as well as letters. Attracting more mail volume must be predicated on meeting these two service standards—high reliability as to day of delivery and faster delivery of all types (classes) of mail. Such service standards, of course, were adopted long ago by Federal Express and UPS. These two service standards can be met in several ways (some of which have already been discussed above).

First, the postal service should process each piece or batch of mail at each step of its journey by the predetermined time necessary to get that mail delivered on time. This would require some overtime pay and extra peak-time labor to meet these deadlines; however, with proper scheduling and moment-by-moment operations control, these costs should not be excessive. Moreover, these costs should be more than offset by the incremental revenue generated by providing more reliable service than is now offered. More reliable mail service would make history of that worn-out joke, "The check is in the mail."

Second, the postal service should commit to non–first class mailers, such as advertisers, that pieces of mail scheduled for delivery on a certain day will in fact be delivered on that day, provided that this mail is delivered to the postal service by a predetermined number of days in advance of the scheduled delivery date. In particular, this will generate increased volume from retailers who must precisely schedule the arrival of sales announcements and other time-sensitive materials. With flexible labor, greater off-peak utilization of sorting facilities, and good operations control, the postal service could meet scheduled delivery dates with a high degree of reliability.

Finally, the postal service should use a national air hub, and make business deliveries before 9:00 a.m. to draw substantial business-to-business mail volume from Federal Express, private delivery services, and even some electronic data retrieval services (electronic data retrieval can be quite expensive because of telephone line charges).

An aggressive marketing strategy to increase business volume should include attracting additional direct mail business, minimizing mailer costs, and pricing to stimulate the demand for delivery of small parcels.

To build its advertising volume by increasing the number of direct mail pieces sent through the postal system, a private postal service should work to build a more favorable image for direct mail so that the public will be less inclined to think of it as "junk mail." This would take several years to accomplish. In addition, it should develop a pricing structure that would build advertising volume in

125

such a manner as to generate substantial incremental profits. Also, it should recruit a sales force to solicit direct mail business in the same manner that newspapers, magazines, and radio and television stations sell space and time to commercial advertisers.

Active solicitation of direct mail business, coupled with the service and reliability improvements discussed above, should generate a substantial increase in mail volume. Delivering just one more piece of mail a day to every home and business in the United States would boost mail volume by 22 percent, or 35 billion pieces annually. If this additional volume were priced at the average rate for third class (advertising) mail, 11.5 cents per piece in 1988, the postal service would generate incremental revenues of $4 billion. Given that the handling costs of this type of mail would be relatively low, incremental profits would be high. For instance, if this mail could be handled for an incremental cost, before being delivered, of 3 cents per piece (not unfeasible if it were presorted in delivery sequence or were delivered to all mail delivery points within a designated area), then the incremental profit of this mail would be almost $2.9 billion. This figure compares quite favorably with USPS's $13.2 billion cost in 1988 for transporting, sequencing, and delivering the mail, and USPS' average $130 million annual operating *loss* over the last five years.

To minimize mailer costs a private postal service should eliminate onerous and bureaucratic rules and regulations that unnecessarily raise mailer costs or make using direct mail difficult, or both. For instance, direct mail advertisers should be able to mail an advertising circular to every addressee on a certain mail route or in certain city blocks without having to put a mailing label on each piece. The Direct Mail Marketing Association and other trade associations can undoubtedly provide many other suggestions as to how direct mail volume could be increased.

The postal service's pricing structure should promote the mailing of lightweight, nonbulky items that can easily be delivered by mail carriers rather than by a separate parcel post delivery service. This would entail relatively low rates per ounce, for packages of up to two or three pounds, provided these parcels did not exceed certain size requirements.

Financing the Privatization Transaction

Although USPS reported $34.7 billion in assets at the end of a recent fiscal year (September 30, 1988), the book value of USPS's operating assets is much smaller—about $11.6 billion. The pro forma balance sheet for USPS (Table 12.1) shows the effect of eliminating two major USPS liabilities—retirement benefits and workers' compensation claims—and, dollar-for-dollar, their related assets.

USPS reported a *negative* net worth of $460 million as of September 30, 1988. But USPS's real estate, which has an original cost of $7.25 billion, now has a market value of $10 billion, according to USPS. This market value is probably at least $4 billion more than the depreciated book value of this real estate.

USPS has one interesting financing advantage: $6.14 billion of its liabilities are interest-free. These interest-free liabilities, which arise out of USPS's operating activities, finance a substantial portion of its operating assets. Operating liabilities as of September 30, 1988, included prepaid postage ($1.2 billion), deferred revenue ($787 million), outstanding money orders ($436 million), accrued compensation and employee benefits ($1.96 billion), accounts payable and accrued expenses ($854 million), and employees' accumulated leave ($883 million). Thus, a substantial portion of a private postal service's financing already is permanently in place.

As the lower portion of Table 12.2 shows, approximately $10.1 billion would have to be raised over three years in the private sector to finance the privatization of USPS. The financing would comprise a mix of debt and equity capital. It would be reasonable to expect to sell $3 billion in stock to postal employees and to an ESOP. This proposed financing assumes that USPS's real estate would be acquired at current market values, all of USPS's borrowings from the Federal Financing Bank (in effect, the U.S. Treasury) would be repaid, and capital outlays during the first three years of private ownership would total $6 billion. The privatized postal service would have to generate a pretax income of $1.5 billion annually in order to attract $10.1 billion in capital. This earnings requirement, which equals 4.2 percent of USPS's 1988 revenues, should not be difficult to achieve, given the tremendous opportunities that exist for a privatized postal service to trim costs and raise volume.

While putting firm numbers on the elements of the USPS privatization transaction is not yet possible, Table 12.2 sets out one possible financing structure. Four aspects of a privatization transaction warrant discussion.

First, the cost of liquidating existing, unfunded pension liabilities and workers' compensation claims could have a tremendous impact

Table 12.1

UNITED STATES POSTAL SERVICE
PRO FORMA BALANCE SHEET THAT REFLECTS STRIPPING OUT
OF PENSION AND WORKERS' COMPENSATION LIABILITIES
September 30, 1988
(dollars in millions)

	As reported	Eliminations	Restated
ASSETS			
Cash and securities	$ 3,947	$ 2,718[1]	$ 1,229
Receivables—net	622		622
Supplies and prepaid expenses	163		163
Total current assets	4,732	2,718	2,014
Other assets	13		13
Fixed assets:			
Land	1,038		1,038
Buildings	6,210		6,210
Equipment	4,082		4,082
Less depreciation	(3,529)		(3,529)
Net real estate and equipment	7,801		7,801
Construction in progress	1,527		1,527
Leasehold improvements—net	209		209
Net fixed assets	9,537		9,537
Deferred retirement costs	20,390	20,390	–0–
Total assets	$34,672	$23,108	$11,564
LIABILITIES AND EQUITY CAPITAL			
Current liabilities	$ 5,500		$ 5,500
Long-term debt, noncurrent portion	5,613		5,613
Other liabilities:			
Retirement benefits	19,741	$19,741	–0–
Employees' accumulated leave	883		883
Workers' compensation claims	3,367	3,367	–0–
Other	30		30
Total other liabilities	24,020	23,108	913
Equity capital:			
Capital contributed by government	3,039		3,039
Cumulative deficit since 7-1-71	(3,499)		(3,499)
Net equity capital	(460)	–0–	(460)
Total liabilities and equity	$34,672	$23,108	$11,564

[1]Equal workers' compensation claims less extent to which reported deferred retirement costs exceed reported retirement benefits. These eliminations in effect assume that (a) workers' compensation claims would be fully funded with excess cash in USPS, and (b) the acquirer of USPS would retain the differential between deferred retirement costs and retirement benefits.

Table 12.2

UNITED STATES POSTAL SERVICE
POSSIBLE FINANCING STRUCTURE FOR A PRIVATIZATION TRANSACTION
(dollars in millions)

Uses of funds:

Purchase of USPS operating assets at book value, based on Table 12.1 (restated balance sheet as of 9-30-88)	$11,560
Purchase price premium paid to U.S. Treasury	3,000[1]
Less assumption of all operating liabilities except $5.59 billion of federal financing (probably not assumable)	(6,430)
Net purchase price of operating assets	8,130
Prospective capital outlays during the first three years after privatization to begin implementing the operating improvements outlined in the third section of this paper	6,000
Severance and contract termination costs	1,000
Cost of liquidating USPS's existing pension liabilities and workers' compensation claims in excess of amounts carried on USPS's balance sheet (assumed to be zero)	–0–
Total uses of funds	$15,130

Sources of funds:

Proceeds from selling excess fixed assets	$ 2,000
Excess cash in USPS on acquisition date	1,000
Depreciation cash flow during the first three years of private ownership	2,000
Permanent financing:	
Sale of stock to USPS employees and to a postal ESOP (assumed to average $4,000 per employee)	3,000
Sale of stock and debt to institutions and to the general public	7,130
Total permanent financing	10,130
Total sources of funds	$15,130

[1]Price premium equals the excess of the market value of real estate over depreciated cost (estimated to be $4.5 billion) minus severance and contract termination costs (estimated to be $1 billion) and minus the negative net equity of the USPS on September 30, 1988 ($460 million).

on the price paid for USPS's operating assets, and possibly make or break the transaction by virtue of the enormity of these numbers. The unfunded pension liability could possibly be reduced, however, by offering postal employees the opportunity to purchase a substantial portion of the stock in the privatized postal service at some discount from market value (this opportunity is discussed below).

Second, USPS owns or leases substantial amounts of unused or underutilized real estate. Improvements in operating efficiency should make numerous assets redundant. As a result, liquidating a substantial portion of USPS's real estate at a premium over book value, and possibly in excess of appraised values, should be possible.

Third, the transaction should include financing to permit $6 billion of capital investment over the first three years following privatization. A substantial portion of these funds would be invested in equipment that would improve productivity and provide for better service.

Finally, there are numerous reasons why USPS employees should become substantial stockholders in a private postal service. Some of them are as follows: ownership participation will give postal employees an incentive to support productivity improvements, specifically the increased use of part-time employees as attrition reduces the number of full-time employees; stock becomes an important bargaining chip in reducing unfunded pension liabilities; and employees represent a substantial, built-in source of equity capital for the new entity.

Dealing with Opponents of Privatization

There are a number of stakeholders who will oppose privatization of the Postal Service. They include: postal employees; postal labor union leaders; postal management; competitors; magazine, newspaper, and Yellow Pages publishers; radio and television stations; airlines; contract truckers; suppliers and contractors; direct mail houses and mailing-list brokers; small towns and villages with post offices; and Congress. The following outlines how to deal with each of these opponents.

Postal employees are a very likely source of opposition, particularly because they will fear massive layoffs and wage give-backs.

Rural letter carriers may offer especially strong opposition to privatization, as they will fear the end of rural mail delivery. However, postal employees should favor privatization if they can see an economic gain for themselves. In addition, they should value the more enlightened management and improved working conditions that almost surely will evolve with privatization.

Postal labor union leaders strongly oppose privatization because they see it as a threat to their power. This is an understandable concern because more flexible manning standards, relaxed work rules, and profit incentives for their rank-and-file members will reduce labor-management antagonisms and thus weaken the postal unions. Overcoming union leader opposition should be possible, however, if the privatization proposal is sufficiently attractive to the union membership. If privatization is properly "sold" to postal employees, their union leaders will have no choice but to go along with it.

Granting postal workers the right to strike would help win over union leaders. As obnoxious as the right to strike may seem, United Parcel Service has survived several strikes, and probably is stronger today for having experienced them.

Postal management should generally be supportive of privatization, particularly because of greater earnings potential and more latitude to function as managers. Postmasters, particularly in the smaller post offices, however, may view privatization as a device to reduce their status and compensation. On September 30, 1988, USPS employed 27,774 postmasters.

Competitors, specifically Federal Express and United Parcel Service, may strongly oppose privatization since a privatized postal service will be a much more energetic and effective competitor than USPS. To the extent that competitors oppose privatization, efforts will have to be made to highlight the self-interest of this opposition.

United Parcel Service's opposition might be muted if it could see benefits for itself in postal privatization. One potential area of cooperation with United Parcel Service—the postal service would act as a retail gatherer of larger parcels for United Parcel to deliver—was discussed earlier. Another area of profitable cooperation might be some sort of shared delivery service in extremely remote areas, such as Alaska, southern Utah, eastern Nevada, and like areas. Also, United Parcel Service might not be too unhappy to lose to a postal service the delivery of very small parcels.

Opposition from Federal Express and other overnight delivery services could be muted if Express Mail was discontinued or divested from the Postal Service as part of the privatization process. USPS probably loses money on Express Mail, so getting rid of it would make good economic sense. However, the more important reason to dump Express Mail is to end its diversion of management talent from the Postal Service's main job of delivering the regular mail.

Newspaper and magazine publishers will oppose privatization on the grounds that it will bring higher postage rates for newspapers and magazines, and thus circulation declines, erosion of the First Amendment, and eventually the collapse of the Republic. Although postal rates for publications may or may not increase after privatization, privatization's real threat will be to the advertising revenues of newspapers, magazines, and the Yellow Pages, not to circulation.

Given that the postal system is underdeveloped as an advertising medium (i.e., direct mail), a privatized postal system should, and almost certainly will, aggressively seek to build its direct mail revenues. It can do so, particularly in the large metropolitan areas, through its unsurpassable capability of delivering advertising messages into very precisely defined areas. Regional issues of newspapers and magazines cannot begin to match the targeting capability of a postal service. The postal system now has that capability, although bureaucratic rules have greatly crippled it. Small merchants, in particular, would value the opportunity to deliver their messages within small, targeted areas at reasonable cost. Highly localized direct mail also would give these advertisers a cost-effective alternative to the extremely high Yellow Pages advertising rates charged in large metropolitan areas.

A vigorous postal service would be particularly effective in cutting into the advertising revenues of both central city and suburban newspapers. Thus, high-minded newspaper and magazine opposition to privatization will have to be shown to be blatant self-interest. Television may prove to be the best medium with which to convey that message.

Some radio stations, possibly those in small and medium size cities, might feel some effect from postal privatization; however, the effect should not be particularly severe. Television advertising revenues will be least affected by privatizing the postal service.

132

Airlines probably would object to privatization, or more specifically, to a national air hub, if in fact they still make money by
hauling mail. Given the tumult of deregulation and recent changes
in air mail contracting procedures, this is an issue that needs closer
analysis.

Much intercity mail moves in trucks owned and operated by
independent truckers who are under contract to USPS. Thirteen
thousand such contracts are in existence. Establishing a national air
hub would reduce the amount of mail moved by trucks, particularly
mail moving between 300 and 600 miles. Also, a private postal
service might find it more desirable to operate its own trucks with
its own employees. Thus, contract truckers probably would object
strongly to privatization. But their opposition could be tempered
by phasing out contract trucking over several years and offering to
hire these truckers and to buy their equipment at fair market values.

Many existing suppliers and contractors to USPS, particularly
firms that specialize in serving the Postal Service, properly would
fear changes in well-established relationships. They possibly could
be won over to privatization with the message that an invigorated,
growing postal service would generate even larger sales for these
firms.

Direct mail houses and mailing-list brokers could easily fear that a
simpler, more marketing-oriented direct mail program, particularly
one that reduced the need for mailing labels, might reduce their
business. But these firms actually should benefit overall from efforts
to boost the attractiveness of direct mail as an advertising medium.

Small towns and villages now on the map would have two fears
about privatization. One, their town or village would cease to exist
as a place if they lost their Zip Code and thus their name no longer
appeared in postal directories. Second, they would lose their post
office. Properly managed, each of these fears can be put to rest
quite easily.

First, there is no reason why every crossroads hamlet in America
cannot be listed in the National Five-Digit ZIP Code and Post Office
Directory. Some of these hamlets might share a ZIP Code with
another, but at least they would be listed. This would be a minor
cost to a private postal service.

Second, the concept of post office franchising should be
expanded (it now exists in a limited manner through contract

133

branches and stations). This would pave the way for replacing many small, low-revenue-producing post offices with the franchised offering of postal services through various types of retail outlets. Banks and bank branches in small towns would be natural candidates for post office franchises, as would office supply stores and newsstands, or even 7-Elevens. Through post office franchising the number of postal outlets in the rural regions of the country as well as in urban areas could actually be expanded. Employees at current small post offices could be shifted to the new franchised post offices.

The House and Senate committees that deal with postal matters quite likely would object to losing the rest of their already declining political power over the postal system. Because postal matters have been of decreasing concern to Congress since 1970, however, the institutional interest of Congress would not likely be a major roadblock to privatization.

Sources of Support for Privatization

Sources of support for privatizing the Postal Service include the general public, businesses, state and local governments, and advocates of reducing the size of the federal government.

Absolutely key to privatizing the Postal Service, of course, is winning the support of the 98.5 percent of all American adults whose only contact with USPS is as a customer. This support should be built on four commitments by the organizers of postal privatization.

First, first class postage, for the first five or ten years following privatization, will not rise more than 80 percent of the Consumer Price Index. In effect, a commitment would be made to reduce slightly the real cost of mailing a letter to Aunt Nellie.

Second, delivery reliability will be improved as the flow of mail quickens. Specifically, this would entail a commitment to reach, within five years, 98 percent delivery reliability and two-day first class delivery anywhere in the continental United States.

Third, wider availability of retail postal services should be coupled with evening and weekend hours where appropriate.

Finally, delivery will be made to the household door for those who now receive their mail at outside "cluster boxes." Cluster boxes, which substitute for delivery to individual homes, merely are an aggregation of individual mailboxes at one location. They are comparable to mailboxes in the lobby of an apartment house. While clusters of mailboxes are acceptable inside apartment houses, they are unsatisfactory delivery points for townhouses and individual houses.

The general public has probably become more accepting of a private, competitive postal service in the last 10 years, as UPS has become practically ubiquitous and as Federal Express, through its television ads, has made most adult Americans aware of yet another alternative to USPS.

Most business mailers should support privatization once they are sold on what its payoff will be for them. The commitment to hold price increases on first class mail below the rate of inflation should have broad appeal, since most businesses primarily use first class mail. Faster and more reliable delivery service will be a big seller, along with a commitment to achieving letter delivery almost anywhere in the United States by 9:00 a.m. of the second business day.

Privatization also should appeal to many, but not necessarily all, specialized business mailers. Advances in sorting automation should enable a private postal service to gradually reduce real postage costs for large first class mailers such as utilities, banks, and retailers. Competitive pricing and reliable delivery of small parcels will give many mailers a viable alternative to United Parcel Service. Many time-sensitive mailers will find *reliable* two-day first class mail service to be an acceptable alternative to Federal Express in many instances, and even to the fax machine in some cases. Direct mailers, and potential direct mailers such as small merchants, will value the reduced costs and greater reliability of advertising mailings coupled with an effort to build a positive image for advertising mail.

Privatization of the Postal Service would most likely increase the amount of taxes paid by the service, directly or indirectly, to state and local governments. They, along with other mailers, also would benefit from improved postal services.

Advocates of shrinking the size of the federal government should, of course, favor Postal Service privatization, particularly since USPS employees now represent over one-fourth of the federal civilian work force. Unfortunately, the privatization of USPS will not have a significant impact on the budget deficit. Under governmental accounting rules, privatization might account for a one-time gain to the federal government of as much as $3 billion. Privatization of the USPS pension obligation also might contribute to deficit reduction. Longer term, however, privatization would turn the Postal Service from a drain on the federal budget to a not-insignificant payer of federal taxes.

Issues a Privatization Proposal Must Address

Major issues that must be addressed to privatize the Postal Service include: employee pensions and unfunded pension benefits; accrued workers' compensation liabilities; universal delivery service; differential pricing; subsidized classes of mail; the first class mail monopoly; regulation; and postal inspectors and privacy issues.

The issue of employee pensions and any unfunded pension benefits was raised above. The retirement benefits shown as a USPS liability in Table 12.1 ($19.74 billion) represent an unfunded pension liability owed by USPS to the U.S. Civil Service Retirement and Disability Fund (the Fund). This unfunded liability relates to pay increases above a basic postal wage level. The USPS pension obligation for the basic postal wage level is substantially funded. Deferred retirement costs ($20.39 billion), the related asset shown in Table 12.1, represents the present value of payments the USPS is scheduled to make to the Fund over the next 30 years to fully fund its retirement benefits liability. In its fiscal year that ended September 30, 1988, the USPS paid $1.568 billion to the Fund to reduce its retirement benefits liability.

As discussed above, it should be possible to negotiate a reduction in the retirement benefits liability (and a corresponding reduction in the deferred retirement costs asset) in exchange for a preferential price on the stock sold to USPS employees in a privatization transaction. This tradeoff could substantially reduce the $1.568 billion the USPS must now contribute annually to the Fund and also absorb as an operating expense. In effect, postal employees would exchange the certainty of a portion of their eventual pension payment for stock that might be worth substantially more by the time they retire.

The substantial obligation of accrued workers' compensation liabilities should be funded as part of a privatization transaction so as to remove this liability from the balance sheet of a private postal

136

service. Table 12.1 shows that a portion of USPS's excess cash could be used to fund this obligation. Using some of USPS's cash for this purpose would still leave USPS with over $1 billion in cash, which is more than enough to meet its normal operating needs. Also, excessively liberal aspects of the workers' compensation program for postal employees must be tightened up as part of the privatization process.

Universal delivery service—maintaining postal service to all present addresses, particularly in the rural areas—should be guaranteed; in fact, the recent attempt by USPS to boost efficiency at addressees' expense by delivering mail to cluster units should be reversed as part of a commitment to offering better service. For marketing reasons, above all, a private postal service must serve every single address in the United States. United Parcel Service voluntarily does so in the 48 continental states. The postal service marketing message would be both stronger and simpler if no delivery exceptions had to be pointed out. It is good business, as well as good politics, to guarantee universal mail service.

Differential pricing, with some paying more than others for a given service, is an economist's dream, but largely impractical in a high-volume, low-unit-price operation such as a postal service pursuing increased automation. Differential pricing theoretically can be justified under three circumstances—as a function of distance, cost of delivery, and weight.

Distance, as such, does not add much to the cost of delivering first class mail since most postal costs are incurred in collecting, sorting, and delivering mail, and in the retail and administrative functions that support those activities. For a typical half-ounce first class letter, the cost differential between local delivery and cross-country delivery most likely does not exceed two cents. In congested urban areas, moving a letter across town might cost more than moving it from Albany to Sacramento. Given the problems and costs of administering rate differentials based on cost, a distance-based rate differential probably is not worthwhile. Federal Express's rates reflect only weight and speed of delivery, not distance, except on shipments to Hawaii and Alaska.

Rate differentials based on cost of delivery usually assume that it costs more to deliver mail to rural addressees than it does to urban addressees. Differences in delivery costs, however, are certainly more complicated than this assumption. In any case, varying postal rates on the basis of cost of delivery is even less feasible than it is to base them on distance traveled.

Weight always has been, and reasonably would continue to be, a basis for varying postage charges.

The issue of mail subsidies divides into two segments—cross-subsidization (i.e., from one mail user to another) and cash subsidies from the U.S. Treasury. Unfortunately, USPS is laced with both types of subsidies, although cash subsidies paid out of the Treasury have been declining as a percentage of total USPS revenues.

Competitive pressures will keep cross-subsidization to a minimum in a private postal service. Therefore, imposing cross-subsidization requirements on the postal service would be no more tolerable than imposing such requirements on the telephone companies and other private utilities. In other words, publications and non-profit, political, and other special interest mailers should not be subsidized by all other mailers by virtue of the type of organization they represent.

A three-part strategy should be adopted to minimize the imposition of cross-subsidization requirements. First, the downside of cross-subsidies (i.e., poor service) should be pointed out to the beneficiaries of these subsidies; second, the price paid for USPS's operating assets should be appropriately reduced by the present value of any cross-subsidization requirements imposed on a private postal service. Finally, all mandated cross-subsidization requirements should be phased out over a five- to ten-year period.

Cash subsidies from the Treasury are ultimately a federal budget decision. The blind, libraries, nonprofit organizations, and other worthies would receive reduced postage rates only to the extent that Congress was willing to appropriate funds to cover the cost of these rate subsidies. As a practical matter, most nonprofit charities and religious groups will sooner or later have to pay the same postage rates as do for-profit mailers. Telephone rates, of course, do not reflect the profit orientation of the user.

USPS has fought tenaciously to preserve its first class mail monopoly, as granted under the private express statutes. This has been a mistake because this monopoly offers no benefits, only disadvantages. Thus, a private postal service should disclaim any interest in any type of postal monopoly.

138

There are several reasons for avoiding the burden of a mail monopoly. First, disclaiming any interest in perpetuating the first class mail monopoly will greatly undercut opposition to privatization, particularly from those who have other reasons for opposing privatization. Second, offering to compete without any grant of monopoly powers will almost totally obliterate any rationale for regulating postal rates and services. This would give the private postal service the same rate and service flexibility that UPS and Federal Express now enjoy. Third, imposing cross-subsidy requirements on a private postal service possessing no monopoly powers will be more difficult legislatively. It would be no more feasible politically to do so than to impose similar requirements on United Parcel Service and Federal Express. Fourth, special-interest groups will be much less able to use the political process to impose restrictions on a private postal service that has escaped regulation by virtue of not possessing any monopoly powers. Finally, the threat of competition will continually maintain pressure on postal management and labor to keep costs down and service quality up.

While a private postal service may suffer occasionally from cream-skimming, such as when the local Boy Scout troop delivers Christmas cards or when an entrepreneur delivers local utility bills or advertising circulars, as a practical matter, the existing postal service, *run in an efficient and reliable manner*, comes as close to being a natural monopoly as one can get. While some might not agree, it would be almost impossible to profitably operate a second, universal postal service. Further, natural monopolies, by their very definition, do not need legal protection. Thus, there is no genuine need to keep the private express statutes once the postal service is privatized.

Furthermore, it is important to keep any natural monopoly on its toes. Thus, there always must be the possibility, and the occasional reality, for competitors to find and attempt to capitalize on its weaknesses. Never-ending attacks on whatever natural monopoly the postal service has will do much to maintain the quality and efficiency of its service and to minimize cross-subsidies within its pricing structure.

The following are key to maintaining the near-natural monopoly of a postal system: (1) reliable, predictable delivery service; (2) ease in depositing mail into the postal service, which means having lots of collection boxes and good pick-up services for mass mailers; and (3) building postal volume so as to reduce unit delivery costs.

Only UPS comes close, in the form of offering a national delivery service, to matching USPS's delivery capabilities. Yet UPS lacks, and probably always will lack, two essential elements that give a postal service its likely natural monopoly: daily delivery service to every door and more than 400,000 mail collection boxes, many of which are accessible 24 hours a day. Thus, even UPS is unlikely to ever compete directly against a universal door-to-door postal system.

It is of paramount importance to the success of a private postal service that regulation, to the extent it would be necessary, be minimal and comparable to that imposed on its competitors. Abolition of the Postal Rate Commission should accompany the privatization of the postal service as postal service regulation should not include rate-setting.

With respect to postal inspectors and postal privacy issues, the mails should enjoy the same privacy as do telephone conversations. Law enforcement authorities and government intelligence agencies should have no more access to the mails than they do to electronic communications. By the same measure, a private postal service should no more attempt to censor what is sent through the mails by consenting adults than what is uttered by consenting adults during telephone conversations.

On the other hand, a private postal service must protect the mail, while it is in the service's possession, from theft and diversion. The postal service also has the right to stop people from using the mails to defraud other people. The existing Postal Inspection Service should be limited to just these two functions; the investigatory and arrest powers of the postal inspectors should be no more than what is necessary to protect the mails and prevent their fraudulent use.

Conclusion

As this chapter has attempted to argue, privatizing USPS is feasible and desirable from both economic and public welfare perspectives. Although there are many political roadblocks to privatization, the potential benefits justify substantial investment in eventually achieving that privatization.

13. The Federal Role in Postal Services and Opportunities for Privatization

Carol Crawford

This is a review of the Federal role in postal services and of current opportunities for privatizing key functions of the United States Postal Service. The provision of postal services is a natural candidate for privatization. Postal services are user funded; the user charges of the USPS nearly cover its costs. While the annual federal subsidy to the USPS has a significant budgetary impact, it is relatively small compared to total USPS expenses. The subsidy itself is a separate issue from privatization. Finally, the USPS is not a natural monopoly; some of its activities are very successfully and profitably replicated by the private sector.

Following a brief overview, the paper first describes and analyzes three proposals to privatize the USPS generally, and then discusses specific functions of the USPS and arguments for and against privatization of those functions.

Overview

The Structure and Activities of the United States Postal Services

The Postal Reorganization Act of 1970 converted the Post Office Department into the USPS, an independent establishment run on a business-like basis within the executive branch. The USPS commenced operations July 1, 1971.

The USPS is governed by an 11-member Board of Governors appointed by the president, a postmaster general who is selected by the governors, and a deputy postmaster general who is selected by the governors and the postmaster general. Decisions on changes in domestic rates of postage and fees for postal services are recommended to the governors of the USPS by the independent Postal

The author was associate director of the U.S. Office of Management and Budget. This paper was submitted to the President's Commission on Privatization.

Rate Commission after a hearing on the record under the Administrative Procedure Act. The commission also recommends decisions on changes in the domestic mail classification schedule to the governors. Decisions of the governors on postage rates, fees for postal services, and mail classification are final, although subject to judicial review.

Postal activities include mail processing, delivery, and transportation; customer services; research and development; administration of postal field activities; and associated expenses of providing facilities and financing. Its three largest functions—mail processing (or sorting), delivery, and customer services (e.g., selling stamps and weighing mail)—could be considered for privatization individually. Together, these three basic USPS functions in 1987 represented 83.1 percent of the total USPS workhours, and the salaries and benefits associated with them were 63.2 percent of total USPS expenses.

USPS activities are financed from the following sources: (1) mail and services revenue; (2) reimbursements from federal and nonfederal sources; (3) proceeds from borrowing; (4) interest from U.S. securities and other investments; (5) appropriations by Congress; and (6) sale or lease income from its properties. The appropriations currently cover amounts for revenue forgone (as a result of the low rates for most religious and charitable mailings), and small amounts for the previous nonfunded workmen's compensation liabilities of the former Post Office Department. Until FY 1981, the federal appropriation also covered so-called public service costs not tied to any particular class of mail. Borrowings are not to exceed $10 billion outstanding at any one time. In any one fiscal year, the net increase in amounts outstanding may not exceed $1.5 billion for capital improvements and $500 million for operating expenses.

An important element of the financial picture of the USPS is the extent and nature of the properties it owns, and the future potential income from these properties. The USPS owns a total of 4,597 properties. The Postal Reorganization Act of 1970 transferred to the USPS, at no cost, 2,250 federal facilities that were more than 55 percent occupied by the Postal Service at that time. (GSA received ownership of the federal facilities in which GSA occupied more than 45 percent.) Some of the USPS properties (300 to 500, or around 10 percent) are older, underutilized two- and three-story buildings in prime commercial locations. The USPS currently collects $25 million annually in lease income from the commercial development of its facilities, and substantial amounts of additional revenue could be generated from the further commercial development of these properties.

Recent Trends in the USPS Budget

The accompanying figures depict important financial and other trends of the operations of the USPS.

- Figure 13.1 presents the total expenses and total revenues of the USPS from FY 1977 through FY 1987. The average annual increase in expenses over this period was 7.8 percent, and the average annual increase in revenues was 8.2 percent. In general, revenues start lagging behind expenses until a rate increase is implemented, and then revenues exceed expenditures for a time.

- Figure 13.2 presents the net income or loss in fiscal years 1977 through 1987. This amount has ranged from a net loss of $695 million for FY 1977 to a net income of $1.1 billion for FY 1982. While the year-end result has seemed to vary widely, it should be noted that FY 1977's net loss represented only 4.5 percent of total expenses that year, and the net income for FY 1982 was 4.9 percent of that year's total expenses.

- Figure 13.3 shows the trend in compensable workyears from FY 1978 through FY 1987. The USPS is a labor-intensive operation, with around 80 percent of its costs labor-related. Compensable workyears are the sum of the total number of permanent positions and the full-time equivalents for other positions (e.g., part-time and temporary positions) and for overtime and holiday pay. Compensable workyears rose from 650,000 in FY 1978 to 805,000 in FY 1987, for an average annual increase of 2.4 percent (4.0 percent average annual increase since FY 1983), despite efforts at productivity improvements.

- Figure 13.4 shows the trend in total mail volume from FY 1977 through FY 1987, as well as the trends in the volume of the two largest classes of mail, first class mail (51.2 percent of the total in FY 1987) and third class mail (38.8 percent of the total in FY 1987). Third class mail represents a larger share of the total mail volume than formerly, as it has risen at an annual

143

Figure 13.1

TOTAL USPS EXPENSES AND REVENUES, FY 1977–FY 1987

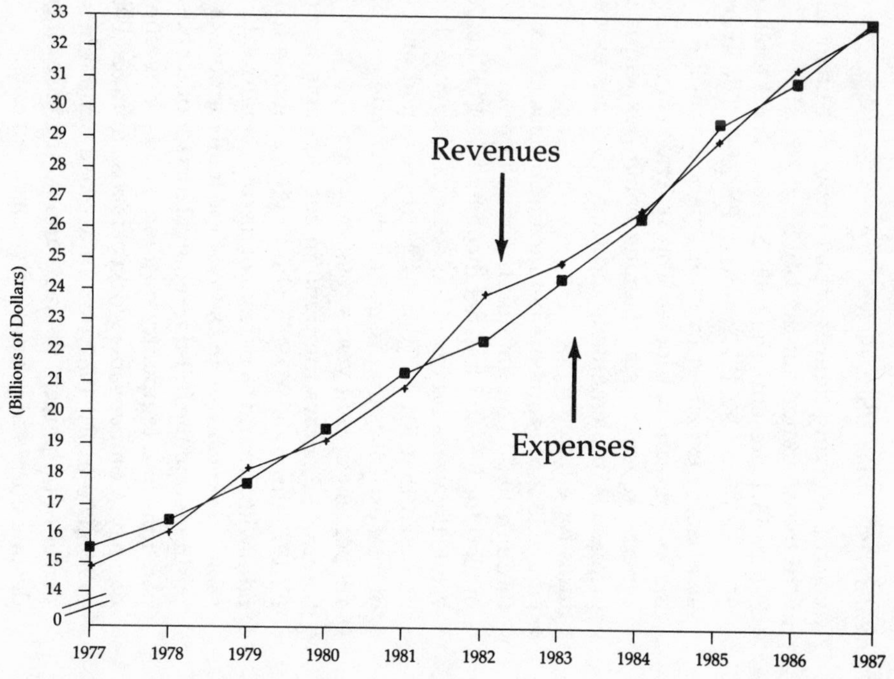

Figure 13.2

USPS Year-End Net Income or Loss, FY 1977–FY 1987

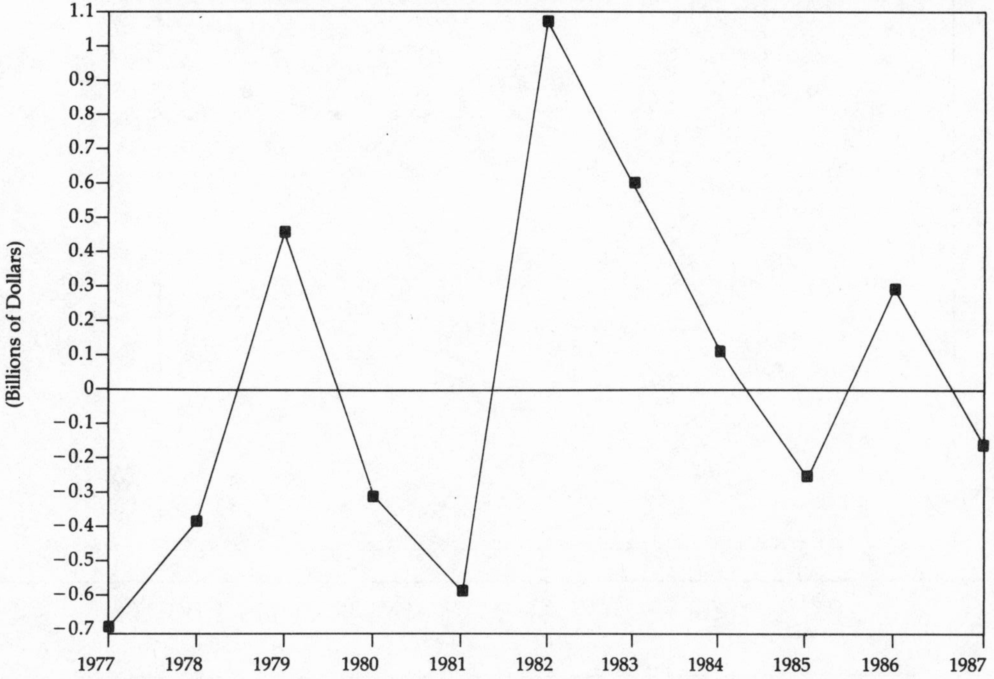

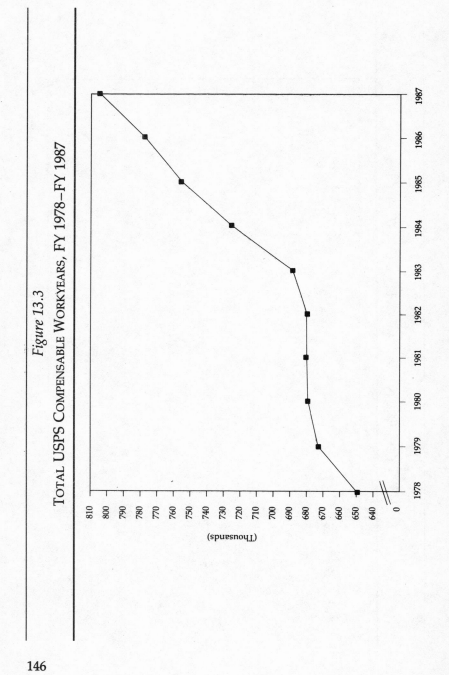

Figure 13.3

TOTAL USPS COMPENSABLE WORKYEARS, FY 1978–FY 1987

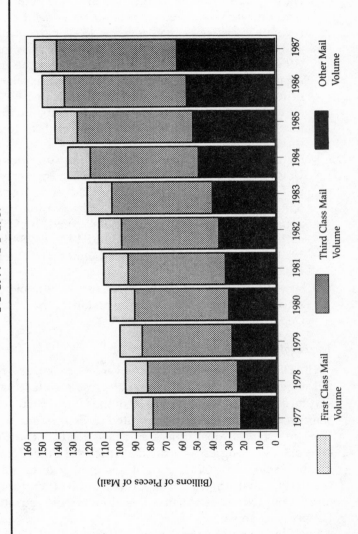

Figure 13.4

TOTAL USPS MAIL VOLUME, FIRST CLASS MAIL VOLUME, AND THIRD CLASS MAIL VOLUME, FY 1977–FY 1987

rate of 9.6 percent, faster than either the total mail volume (which rose 5.3 percent per year on average) or first class mail (which rose an average of 3.9 percent per year).

- Figure 13.5 shows the trends over the same fiscal years in total mail and service revenue (around 95 percent of total USPS revenue), first class mail revenue (59.4 percent of total mail and service revenue in FY 1987), and third class mail revenue (19.4 percent of total mail and service revenue in FY 1987). Again, revenue from third class mail makes up a larger portion of total mail and service revenue than formerly. Its average annual increase has been 13.4 percent, compared to 9.2 percent for first class mail revenue and 9.3 percent for total mail and service revenue.

- Figure 13.6 presents the trend in federal appropriations to the USPS over the FY 1977–FY 1987 period. The sharp reduction in FY 1982 was the result of the end of appropriations for the so-called public service costs. The portion of the annual appropriation for that purpose amounted to $920 million in each of fiscal years 1977, 1978, and 1979; $828 million in FY 1980; $486 million in FY 1981; and ended at $12 million in FY 1982.

- Figure 13.7 shows the trend in the first class mail postage rates since 1968, just before the conversion of the old Post Office Department to the USPS in 1971.

The Legal Monopoly over Postal Services

The USPS has a legal monopoly over letter mail, as a result of the net effect of the so-called private express statutes that comprise several sections of Titles 18 and 39 of the United States code. These statutes arise from the power granted to Congress in the Constitution "to establish post offices and post roads." The Constitution does not give Congress—as did the Articles of Confederation before it—the "sole and exclusive right and power of establishing and regulating post offices." The Constitution, therefore, does not direct Congress to establish a postal monopoly, but it empowers Congress to do so.

Initially, Congress simply went along with the regulations in force under the old Articles of Confederation. In 1792 it passed legislation prohibiting any private persons from carrying "letters"

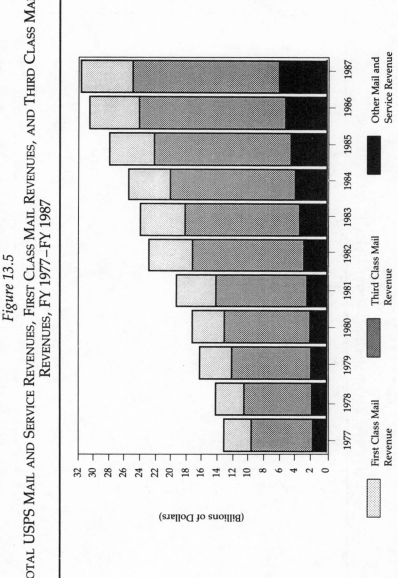

Figure 13.5

TOTAL USPS MAIL AND SERVICE REVENUES, FIRST CLASS MAIL REVENUES, AND THIRD CLASS MAIL REVENUES, FY 1977–FY 1987

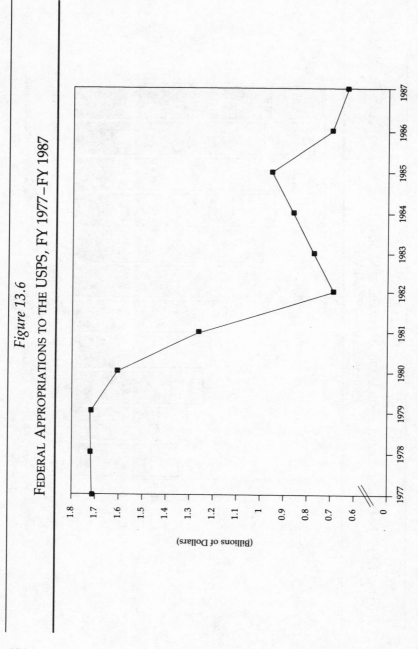

Figure 13.6

FEDERAL APPROPRIATIONS TO THE USPS, FY 1977–FY 1987

150

Figure 13.7
RECENT HISTORY OF POSTAL RATES FOR FIRST CLASS MAIL

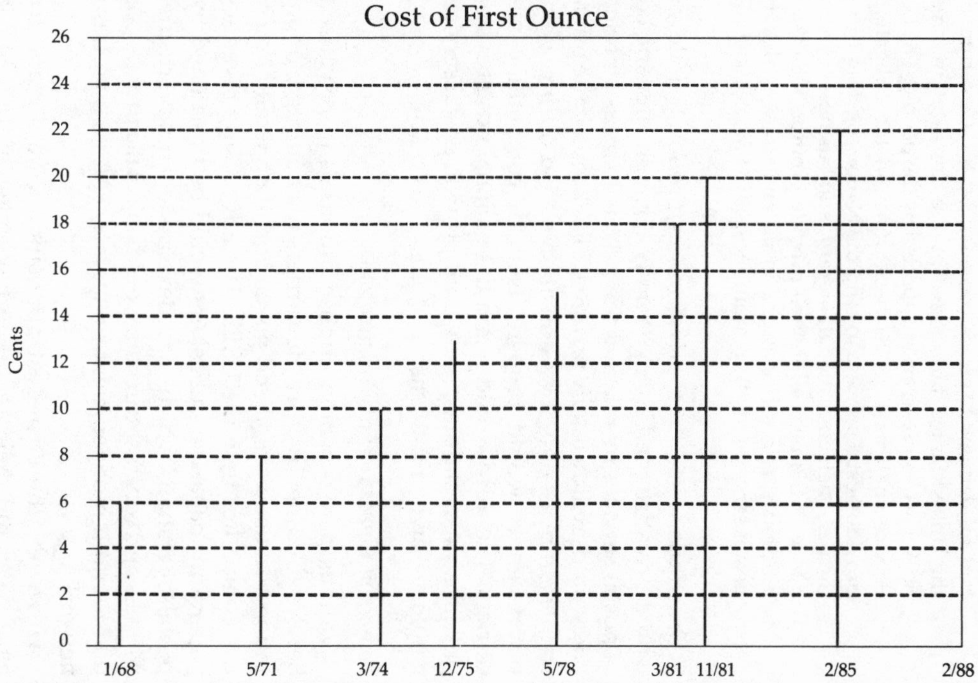

for hire, with an exception for special messengers. The current private express statutes have evolved from this legislation and set forth Congress's postal policy:

> The United States Postal Service shall be operated as a basic and fundamental service provided by the Government of the United States, authorized by the Constitution, created by Act of Congress, and supported by the people. The Postal Service shall have as its basic function the obligation to provide postal services to bind the Nation together through the personal, educational, literary, and business correspondence of the people. It shall provide prompt, reliable, and efficient services to patrons in all areas and shall render postal services to all communities. (Title 39, section 101)

Descriptions of three privatization proposals follow. The first would privatize the USPS generally through allowing competition in postal services by relaxing the private express statutes. The second would create a totally private USPS, keeping the private express statutes in place only for a transition period during which the new private entity would prepare itself for competition with private carriers. The third would retain the national postal system and the private express statutes, but would provide postal services through employee-owned franchises.

Sources of Opposition to Privatization

Various parties would oppose proposals to privatize the Postal Service. Competitive private carriers may strongly oppose privatization because a privatized postal operation would be a more effective competitor than the USPS. The advertising revenues of newspaper and magazine publishers would be threatened by a private postal operation, which may develop as an advertising medium. Airlines and contract truckers would object if a private postal operation found it more efficient to operate with its own transportation network.

However, the strongest opposition would come from postal employees and their unions. A key aspect of the USPS is its labor-intensive operation; around 80 percent of its costs are labor-related. As a result, various privatization or contracting out proposals would have the effect of streamlining the very large work force (around 750,000 employees).

USPS salaries exceed the salaries of comparably skilled private-sector employees by around 20 percent. Moreover, most of the USPS employees have vested rights in the federal retirement systems. Any serious restructuring of the USPS, therefore, is quite likely to warrant the establishment of a displaced-workers program that justly compensates the employees with other employment opportunities or outright payments of some sort.

If major postal operations were to be moved to the private sector, employees could be offered a host of benefits from which to select. For example, a comprehensive list of benefits (e.g., deferral of annuity until retirement, a lump-sum payment for pension benefits, long-term Treasury bonds, and a guarantee of preferential hiring status) could be compiled, with each item assigned a value. Subject to personal preference, tenure, and salary, each employee could select one or more of these items so that the total compensation remained within the bounds of a total separation allowance.

Existing Proposals to Privatize the USPS

Allow Competition by Relaxing the Private Express Statutes

The private express statutes comprise several sections of Titles 18 and 39 of the United States Code. Their net effect is to grant the USPS a legal monopoly over "letter" mail (i.e., first and third class letters). The definition of "letter" is administratively set by the USPS; the statutes somewhat loosely use such terms as "letter," "printed matter," "packet," and "parcel," and give the USPS the authority to define the nature of the items which fall only under the jurisdiction of the USPS. The USPS also has a de facto monopoly over other categories of mail because it is illegal for private carriers to deposit any item in an ordinary household mailbox unless the item has a stamp affixed to it.

Two general ways exist for relaxing the private express statutes and allowing competition. The first is administrative action by the USPS Board of Governors to allow competitors access to the mail by modifying the regulatory definition of "letter." For instance, in 1979 the USPS suspended the application of the private express statutes to "extremely urgent" letters. A letter is considered extremely urgent if the amount paid for private carriage of the letter is the greater of $3 or 10 times the applicable postage for first class

153

mail. Suspension of the statutes in this case accommodated the growth of private carriers such as Federal Express.

The second general way to relax the private express statutes and allow competition is a statutory change that would allow competitors access to the mailbox. The categories of mail that could be delivered privately if this were done include first class utility bills (which could be delivered by the utility companies themselves), weekly and monthly periodicals, and third class unaddressed advertising circulars. There is concern that allowing others access to locked household mailboxes would undermine the security and integrity of the mail. This risk could be avoided by allowing only certain private parties (e.g., utility companies for the delivery of their own bills to their customers and the private carriers of non-profit mail) access to the locked mailboxes.

Relaxing the private express statutes represents an incremental and gradual approach to the privatization of postal services, which should be relatively easy for the USPS and its customers to become accustomed to. Introducing competition into more areas of postal services would also provide incentives for the USPS to improve efficiency and reduce costs. To retain a large share of the market for the services affected by relaxation of the statutes, the USPS would be highly motivated to increase efficiency and reduce costs.

Give Majority Ownership to Postal Employees

The federal government could give a majority of stock in the USPS to its employees. The government could sell the stock it kept at any time, provided that it sold all of its stock within a set period, say, 10 years. The USPS would continue to operate as a regulated monopoly during a transition period of, say, five years. The postal workers would be prohibited from selling their shares during transition. In exchange for a majority of the stock, the postal employees would relinquish their unfunded pension and workers' compensation claims on the federal government.

At the end of the transition period, the statutory monopoly of the USPS would expire and the regulation of USPS rates would end. Competitors could freely enter any area of mail service, the USPS could set its prices without interference from regulators, and the postal workers could sell their stock. The market price of the stock would reflect how the postal workers had prepared the USPS during the transition period to compete against private, unsubsidized firms. If the postal employees failed to make the USPS efficient, they would be penalized through the low price of their stock once they were allowed to trade it. On the other hand, if the employees made the USPS efficient, the price of their shares would contain a premium reflecting the competitive advantage of the USPS over less efficient rivals.

As a variation on this proposal, the federal government would offer each postal employee USPS stock at a discount below its public offer price. The discount would have to be large enough to compensate the employees for two items: (1) the unfunded pension and workers' compensation liabilities of the USPS (to which the employees would relinquish their claims), and (2) the present value of the postal workers' wage premium over wages for comparable jobs in private, competitive industries. If such a public offering had been conducted in 1987, the value per postal employee of the unfunded pension and workers' compensation claims would have been about $3,300. The discounted value of the wage premium over five years could have been another $20,000 or more per employee.

Giving majority ownership of the USPS to postal employees, or selling USPS stock to them at a discount, would provide powerful incentives to improve efficiency and reduce costs. As shareholders, the employees themselves would have a direct stake in the efficiency and profitability of the USPS. Moreover, the federal subsidy that results from the imbalance between USPS income and expenditures would be eliminated, and the USPS would become a taxpayer. (On the other hand, federal subsidies enacted for specific categories of mail or customers would not necessarily end. The federal government could choose to provide such subsidies after the USPS is privatized, as privatization and this sort of subsidy are separate issues.) Sale of the federal government's stock would also raise revenue.

Postal employees would not necessarily be displaced under this approach. Rather, they would be shareholders and employees of the new private entity, which would retain its monopoly position during the transition period. Their eventual status with the private USPS would depend on the needs of the USPS for improvements in efficiency in order to be able to compete effectively once the transition period and the monopoly of the USPS ended.

155

Rural residents would also not be disadvantaged by reduced services or higher rates. While rural post offices might close, their services could easily be provided by rural carriers—on the road—with significant savings. Uniform rates across geographic areas are likely to continue, as the cost of administering multiple rates based on geographical area would probably be too expensive. Moreover, if subsidies were needed for rural service, they could be provided; again, subsidization is a separate issue from privatization.

Convert USPS Operations to Employee Ownership in Stages and Provide Postal Services through Private Franchises

A proposal from the Thomas A. Roe Institute for Economic Policy Studies at the Heritage Foundation calls for the preservation of the national postal system, with postal services being publicly provided but privately produced through employee-owned franchises. The proposal has nine steps:

1. Retain USPS control over postal rates and activities.
2. Freeze USPS hiring for all activities that can be converted to private contracts.
3. Split the postal activities into independent subfunctions. The USPS is a network of hundreds of subunits that are relatively independent functionally and geographically. The units that can be separated should be identified. The size of a unit and the scope of the activity it carries out should depend upon whether the unit could be conveniently split off from the USPS system and operated as a private enterprise.
4. Offer to transfer ownership of these independent units to their employees and management. If a majority consented to the ownership transfer, the unit would be given to the employees and an Employee Stock Ownership Plan (ESOP) would be established. Any postal employee deciding to go private would be guaranteed a position at USPS at any time within five years of joining its ESOP, if the worker changed his or her mind.
5. Award each new private franchise a three- to five-year contract (a "sweetheart deal") with USPS. The price of the contract would be the historic USPS cost for performing these activities, with an adjustment for inflation. Any cost savings would translate directly into profits for the employee shareholders

during the "sweetheart" period. These new firms would also be permitted to venture into other profit-making commercial activities.

6. Honor the acquired pension benefits of all postal employees opting to join an ESOP. Assets transferred from the USPS to each franchise would "buy out" pension obligations. To the extent that the workers' pension rights exceeded the portion of the assets earmarked for their unit, each worker would be issued a bond providing an annuity upon retirement equal to the individual's remaining accumulated pension benefits.
7. Open franchised activities to competitive bidding after the "sweetheart deal" contract expires.
8. Establish a uniform system for reimbursing private franchises.
9. Establish rigid performance standards for each contracted activity. The USPS would continue to be ultimately responsible for assuring the public timely and reliable service. Minimum standards should be based upon the current USPS performance requirements. USPS decisions on annual contract renewals would take into consideration not only price but also the quality of service provided.

A steady conversion to private ownership of smaller, discrete parts of the USPS would not be as threatening as large-scale proposals to sell or transfer ownership of the entire USPS. The national postal system would remain in place and differential pricing would not be introduced. Remote rural residents would not be threatened with unacceptably low service levels or high postal rates. To the extent that the nation-binding function of the postal system remains important and a public USPS is needed, the public provision of postal services by a national system operating through private franchises would meet this objective.

Moreover, postal employees would again not be displaced. They would continue as shareholders or employees of the franchised units. At the same time, the employees would have strong, new incentives as shareholders and as competitive participants in a contracting out system to improve efficiency and reduce costs.

However, piecemeal privatization could interfere with a smooth-running and reliable postal operation. The entire postal operation is very sensitive to even momentary delays in any segment. For this reason, similar private operations, such as Federal Express and

157

United Parcel Service, contract out very few of their operating activities. Providing reliable postal services through separate private franchises would require a level of coordination that would be very difficult to attain, by either the public national postal system or any other entity. Moreover, the federal subsidy would not necessarily be reduced or eliminated, since the proposal would retain a public, national postal system and USPS control over setting rates.

Individual Operations of the USPS Which Could Be Considered for Privatization

Mail Processing

Mail-processing operations of the USPS in 1987 represented 28.5 percent of total USPS workhours; salaries and benefits connected to mail processing were 22.3 percent of total USPS expenditures. The major costs involved in mail processing have to do with labor-intensive aspects, such as sorting. Transportation accounted for only 7 percent of total costs. Virtually all mail cartage, other than pickup and delivery by postal carriers, is already done by private contractors, either truckers or airlines.

In general, mail is collected from mailboxes by postal workers or delivered to the local post office by the public. At the local post office, local-bound mail (mail addressed to five-digit ZIP Codes served by that same local post office) is sorted to the carrier route for delivery. The remainder of the mail is sent to the area's management sectional center.

Management sectional centers are the major mail-processing centers. Since 1978, these centers have done virtually all nonlocal mail sorting. Centralization is required by the high cost of the machines that sort mail of standard size and shape. There are roughly 500 centers in the United States and its territories, ranging in size from 120 to 4,000 employees. A Postal Rate Commission study found the optimal size to be around 1,400 employees. Both much smaller and much larger centers are considerably less efficient.

At a management sectional center, mail is sorted in one of two ways. Either mail is sorted to five-digit ZIP Codes and sent to local post offices in the area, or mail is sorted to the first three digits of the ZIP Code and sent to the corresponding management sectional center elsewhere in the country. Approximately 37 percent of first class mail stays within a center's area; the other 63 percent is transported from one center to another.

Preferred mail generally goes through management sectional centers; bulk or nonpreferred mail generally goes through one of the 21 bulk mail centers throughout the country. In order to qualify for bulk rates, third class mail must be presorted to the first three digits of the ZIP Code which corresponds to a particular management sectional center.

There are exceptions to this general flow of mail. For example, USPS often sends mail trucks directly to major publishers and then transports that mail directly to the management sectional center, to avoid deluging local post offices with a mass of mail that the publisher has already sorted to some level.

Another deviation from the standard pattern occurs in the case of presorted mail, for which various discounts are offered. Major mailers (usually businesses) may send their mail to a private presort company that ships the mail directly to the destination management sectional center after sorting the mail at least to the three-digit level, and often to the five-digit, nine-digit, or carrier-route level. The presort industry handles about 40 percent (8.5 billion pieces) of all the presorted mail. Many private firms presort up to two to three million pieces of mail per evening for such large business mailers.

The USPS mail-processing operations can be easily separated into discrete, independent subfunctions, each of which can be privatized relatively simply. The presort industry provides a clear precedent for the feasibility of separating the USPS mail-processing operations and contracting them out.

Privatizing mail-processing functions would increase the efficiency and lower the cost of the particular subfunction. For example, in order for a private firm to compete successfully for a contract for the work of one or several management sectional centers, it would have to attain and remain at the optimal size for performing the work in question at the lowest cost. If the route chosen for privatization was converting management sectional centers and bulk mail centers to employee-owned franchises, the employees themselves would have a stake in the efficiency and profitability of their center.

However, if the route chosen for privatization was contracting out, savings to the USPS would not automatically result, due to contractual obligations to postal employees which constrain the USPS from reducing the amount of its labor costs quickly. Mail processing also involves expensive letter-sorting machines, which USPS already has. Contracting out could result in costly and inefficient duplication of equipment.

Delivery Services

Delivery services represent 38.2 percent of the total USPS workhours, and the salaries and benefits associated with delivery services are 28.4 percent of the total USPS expenditures. Delivery services are those activities in which the postal carrier picks up the mail (already sorted to the carrier route) from the local post office, sorts it for delivery, and delivers it. There are around 220,000 delivery routes.

Average urban and rural delivery costs do not differ significantly. There may be some exceptionally isolated rural routes where delivery costs are extremely high, but the averages suggest that these are relatively few. (The evidence suggests that urban-rural cross-subsidization is more extensive with respect to post offices—which have to do with customer services—than with respect to delivery.)

Rural carriers and urban carriers perform different functions, are paid on a different basis (urban carriers are paid slightly more), and belong to different trade unions. Urban carriers average about 500 stops per day; rural carriers average about 400 stops per day. Rural carriers not only provide delivery services like their urban counterparts, but also provide many of the retail services normally provided by urban post offices, such as selling stamps and weighing mail.

Many rural routes are served by "star route" carriers, private contractors with exclusive franchises to carry the mails between specific locations on a scheduled basis. The star route carriers number about 5,500 truck drivers for short and long distances and 5,500 rural delivery carriers. The USPS currently contracts out about $1 billion per year (or 3 percent of its $38 billion operation) for delivery services from the star route carriers, who perform transportation, delivery, and retail functions. A typical star route would be in the vicinity of 100–200 miles, with perhaps 100 stops along the way.

Proposals for privatizing delivery services include the following:
- Make greater use of star route carriers for rural delivery.
- In urban areas, contract personnel could be assigned an on- or off-site working area in connection with local post offices. Such

160

personnel could arrange the already-presorted mail into house number and street sequence, and then deliver it.

- Other suggestions would require the relaxation of the constraints on private delivery in the private express statutes: Reduce the urgent-letter rule limitation (i.e., the price that currently defines an urgent letter, allowing private carriage); license or bond select private mail carriers, so that access to the household mailbox is not open to just any carrier; and allow nonprofit or benevolent mailers to deliver certain types of mail (such as holiday greeting cards). In connection with this last proposal, the USPS experiences a peak mail volume during the Christmas holiday season. The public widely believes that mail service deteriorates at this time. The Postal Service could contract out to certain licensed charitable organizations for local delivery of mail during this time.

Mail-delivery routes are discrete, independent units of the operation of the USPS, easy to separate and contract out. The long history of contracting out to star route carriers supports the contracting out of more rural routes to star route carriers and, in addition, the contracting out of discrete urban routes or areas. Star route carriers can save a third of the cost of rural USPS carriers. Introducing more competition into postal services provides incentives for the USPS to improve efficiency and reduce costs.

Since rural star route carriers serve both delivery and retail functions, they obviate the need for rural post offices. As rural postmaster positions become vacant, the positions can be abolished and the star route carriers can provide the retail services.

Moreover, economic analysis suggests that provision of peak-load services tends to be especially costly, particularly if it necessitates investment in peak-load capacity that is underutilized at other times of the year. Permitting private delivery of mail during the Christmas season, for example, would improve efficiency.

Customer Services

Customer services—selling stamps, weighing mail, etc.—represent 16.4 percent of total USPS workhours, and the salaries and benefits connected with customer services were 12.4 percent of total USPS expenditures. The USPS maintains about 29,000 post offices. About 25,000, according to the Postal Rate Commission, are quite small, and essentially function as mailboxes that also sell stamps and weigh packages. Many are small, rural post offices which do not cover their costs. In rural areas, therefore, the rural carrier frequently both delivers mail and provides retail services such as selling stamps and weighing packages.

A GAO study in the early 1980s found that between 10,000 and 20,000 post offices could be eliminated or converted to operations run by local merchants (sometimes with more limited hours) with no loss in service to the customers. Data provided by the Postal Rate Commission suggest that conversion to merchant-run operations, on average, cuts the cost of customer services roughly in half. In a sample of 16 such conversions, the savings in postal costs were extremely high, averaging over 50 percent. Estimates of what the cost savings would have been if the operating hours had been held constant still yielded an average savings of over 30 percent.

Projections of savings from converting post offices to merchant-run operations are largely due to the elimination of unionized postal workers' salaries. However, the 1986 appropriations language specifically prohibits the USPS from considering such conversions. In practice, the USPS apparently does convert or eliminate a small number of rural post offices each year. Its informal policy is generally not to do so unless or until the rural postmaster dies or retires from office.

The customer-services function is perhaps the easiest postal operation to privatize. The rural carrier's performance of retail services along with delivery services sets a precedent for privatizing this function. Unlike the mail-processing function, the performance of customer services does not require any expensive equipment. Private retailers who are already open late could provide extended service hours to customers at little extra cost.

14. An Off-Budget Post Office?

Ronald D. Utt

In negotiations with Congress over the content of the government's FY 1990 budget, President Bush made a significant concession to several of the nation's most powerful trade unions and their congressional supporters: he agreed to remove the United States Postal Service (USPS) from the unified federal budget, thereby effectively freeing it from any government-mandated efficiencies or cost savings. The president made this concession in return for a congressional commitment to achieve a one-third reduction in the approximately $1.5 billion taxpayer subsidy that the USPS hoped to received in FY 1990. Congress and the unions leaped at the opportunity to free the USPS from the last vestige of any external oversight, and proceeded to craft legislation to achieve this objective. But in predictable congressional fashion, the pending legislation excluded the agreed-upon cost savings.

Congressional reasons for removing the USPS from the budget are based on little more than political expediency. By transferring the USPS's expected FY 1990 loss of $1.8 billion to the netherworld of off-budget accounting, the government creates the illusion of a comparable reduction in the deficit without having to adopt any spending cuts or revenue increases. This accounting gimmick is a bad idea and should be opposed unless significant reforms to make the USPS financially independent of the taxpayer and the U.S. Treasury are enacted. The government's unified budget is supposed to be a thorough accounting of its activities and the removal of any program for the purposes of transitory convenience serves only to mislead the public and undermine important principles of full disclosure. As Comptroller General of the United States Charles A. Bowsher recently observed in testimony on the savings and loan bailout:

The author is John M. Olin Distinguished Fellow at the Heritage Foundation.

We are concerned about the growing number of proposals to establish off-budget entities to carry out government functions. These proposals, whose apparent purpose is usually to avoid the discipline required by constrained budget resources, are a serious threat to the integrity of the government's budget and financial management systems. If the proliferation of such entities continues, it will raise grave doubts about the credibility of the government's reports on its financial operations and condition, making it even more difficult for decision makers and the public to understand and deal meaningfully with the overriding problem of the budget deficit.[1]

The rules and principles of federal budgeting are clear on issues of full accountability. The 1967 President's Commission on Budget Concepts stated that a government-related enterprise should be considered off-budget only when it is "completely privately owned."[2] Obviously, the USPS doesn't pass this simple test and the legislative proposals that would move it off budget would also retain explicit federal ownership. But notwithstanding the 1967 commission's budget definitions, federal budgetary treatment of the USPS over the past several decades has been anything but consistent.

Originally included as part of the unified budget when it was created in 1970, then-OMB Director Casper Weinberger consented to moving the USPS off budget in 1973 as part of an effort to "reduce" the deficit. With the USPS then operating at a loss, Weinberger's rationale for change in budgetary treatment was no more noble than that of today's budget negotiators. Until this change, only one federal entity—the Export/Import Bank—had been shifted off budget. But within three years of the USPS shift in status, six more government agencies and programs were removed from the unified budget to create the illusion of deficit reduction and to protect the programs and their privileged beneficiaries from ongoing fiscal oversight. Many fear this trend could arise again, and the

[1]Testimony of Charles A. Bowsher, Comptroller General of the United States, Postal Hearings, "The Budgetary Treatment of the Proposed Resolution Funding Corporation," Friday, May 19, 1989, GAO/T-AFMD-89-8, pp. 1–2.

[2]Report of the President's Commission on Budget Concepts, October 1967, p. 30.

Bush administration's efforts to put the savings and loan bailout off budget is one more violation of the commission's standards.

In 1985, then-OMB Director Stockman, anticipating the Gramm-Rudman legislation that would more expansively define on-budget federal activities, moved the USPS back on the budget, even though the USPS's losses would widen the unified budget's deficit and make his job that much more difficult. His successor, Director James C. Miller III, aggressively defended the on-budget status of the USPS and used it as leverage to impose badly needed reforms on the enterprise. But less than a year later, the Bush administration has consented to a reversal of this policy.

The current USPS budgetary debate has its origin in the 1987 Omnibus Budget Reconciliation Act, which directed the on-budget USPS to cut its bloated costs by $510 million in 1988 and $735 million in 1989. The USPS was strongly opposed to these requirements. Its amateurish attempt to get the public on its side, by cutting service to save the money, backfired and, instead, led the public and Congress to demand reforms in the way the USPS manages its affairs.

Recognizing that pressure to cut costs and increase efficiency would persist as long as the USPS was part of the unified budget, postal management and unions, and their congressional supporters, responded by proposing that the USPS be *excluded* from the unified budget. For the USPS this change would give it the best of all worlds: it would still receive all of its extant benefits—monopoly protection from competition and access to the U.S. Treasury for subsidies and loans—but without the responsibility to behave in a fiscally prudent fashion. It could continue to run a deficit in its operations, but because the deficit would not show up in the unified budget, there would be less pressure from Congress and the president to keep costs under control. Ultimately, these costs would be borne by the mail users and taxpayers.

While the USPS tends to see itself as an independent, businesslike enterprise, it is, as currently structured, an integral part of the federal government. Its board is appointed by the president and approved by Congress, as are the members of the independent Postal Rate Commission that reviews the USPS's rate increases. The USPS receives three forms of direct subsidy from the taxpayer: full payment of retirees' COLA, almost full payment of retirees' health care, and payments to provide subsidized rates for preferred mailers. Combined, these subsidies will amount to nearly $1.5 billion in FY 1990, and are expected to rise to $2.5 billion by 1994.

The USPS has two other open claims on the U.S. Treasury through what are called "transitional" and "public service" appropriations, last used in 1982. The USPS also has the privilege of borrowing up to $10 billion from both the Federal Financing Bank (a part of the U.S. Treasury) and the U.S. Treasury itself, at subsidized interest rates.

Other federal privileges abound. The USPS is exempt from all income taxes—federal, state, and local. It is exempt from local property taxes as well, although it indirectly pays some where it leases facilities. And finally, it gets to decide who can and cannot compete with it by virtue of its authority to interpret the private express statutes, laws which reserve to the USPS the exclusive right to deliver a "letter" and to use the mailbox attached to or incorporated in each private dwelling. Under these statutes, the USPS alone decides when a citizen violates the private express statutes, an infraction that is subject to criminal prosecution.

To accomplish these savings without necessitating a rate increase, the USPS should be instructed to embark on an aggressive financial reform program that includes the contracting out of selective delivery, sorting, and retail functions, and other important changes.

Janitors would be a good place to start. Citing a GAO study, the President's Privatization Commission noted that the cleaning costs for USPS janitors are $1.88 per square foot, whereas private contractors can do the job for $.77 a square foot in USPS buildings of less than 10,000 square feet. The GAO study estimated that a shift to private contractors in the three (of five) regions studied would save $15 million per year. The GAO further estimated cost savings of 20 to 30 percent in buildings over 10,000 square feet. Contracting out the cleaning of these structures would yield annual savings of between $45 and $77 million per year in 1982 dollars.[3] Adjusting the GAO findings for current costs, OBM estimates that $180 million per year would be saved by contracting out all janitoral functions.[4]

[3]"The Postal Service Can Substantially Reduce Its Cleaning Costs," Report by the U.S. General Accounting Office, December 28, 1982, GAO-AMD-882-23, pp. 5, 8.

[4]"U.S. Postal Service Cost Reduction Proposals," Office of Management and Budget, 1988.

Significant savings could also be achieved in USPS retail functions. Of the roughly 29,000 post offices operated by the USPS, the Postal Rate Commission (PRC) contends that 25,000 are little more than mailboxes that sell stamps and perform limited clerical functions. Another 1982 study by the GAO concluded that about 7,000 post offices could be closed or contracted out with no significant deterioration in service.[5] PRC data suggest that the contracting out of such limited service facilities to existing retail stores would be half as costly as having USPS continue to run them. A 1988 analysis by the Office of Management and Budget concluded that $240 billion could be saved annually by contracting out the 7,000 limited-service post offices in rural areas and the 6,200 limited-service post offices in metropolitan areas.[6] At present, there are approximately 1,700 contractor-operated post offices.

To its considerable credit, USPS management attempted to conduct a pilot project that would have allowed Sears Roebuck and Company to offer the full range of retail window services at 12 Sears stores in the Chicago area. Although vigorous objections by the postal unions led to a cancellation of this project, the USPS contends that it is committed to the concept and will pursue similar opportunities in the future. Such demonstration projects should be encouraged and replicated nationwide with other retail establishments. Making greater use of existing retail outlets would save money and provide customers with more convenient hours and locations.

Expanding the use of private contractors (called "star routes") to deliver rural mail would also lead to significant savings. Private contractors presently have about 10 percent of the rural routes. An OMB analysis estimated that $55 million could be saved annually for each additional 10 percent of the rural deliveries that were contracted out.[7] In its March 1988 report, the President's Privatization Commission estimated that as much as $2 billion per year could be saved if all deliveries were contracted out.[8]

[5]Comptroller of the United States, "Replacing Post Offices with Alternative Services, a Debated, but Unresolved Issue," September 2, 1982, GAO report GGD-82-89.

[6]OMB.

[7]OMB.

[8]*Privatization: Toward More Effective Government*, Report of the President's Commission on Privatization, April 1988, p. 121.

A July 1988 study of delivery costs conducted by the Postal Inspection Service, an organization within the USPS, found that deliveries by the postal service's private-contract carriers cost half as much as deliveries performed by USPS employees.[9] The study covered over a thousand rural and city routes at eight of the USPS's 23 Transportation Management Service Centers. Moreover, according to the study, interviews with postal managers found that "most offices rated contract delivery service, attendance, route coverage, customer satisfaction, and security of the mail equal to rural route and city carrier performance."[10] According to John Crutcher of the Postal Rate Commission, delivery cost savings of up to $5 billion would be possible based on the estimated $10 billion now being spent on delivery by the USPS.[11]

Likewise, the use of part-time employees to satisfy peak-load needs could save another $2 billion per year, according to OMB estimates.[12] Currently, part-time and casual labor is limited to no more than 10 percent and 5 percent, respectively, of the USPS work force covered by the collective bargaining agreement. Efforts to remove these limits during the 1987 labor contract negotiations with postal worker unions were unsuccessful, and the limits remain in place.

Another money saver would be to let the private sector begin delivering third class mail to rural addresses. Several firms are eager to offer this service, which the USPS contends it can provide only at steep losses. If others can do it at a profit, the USPS should step aside and let the taxpayer and mail user save some money.

Contracting out the sorting operations of all new mail volume could save as much as $180 million per year.[13] The USPS has already fostered the creation of a private sorting industry by offering $.04 discounts per letter presorted by ZIP Code. This industry could easily expand to do much more. USPS efforts to meet the rising tide of letters through discounts to mailers using letters with bar codes that can be read by optical scanners have not been as successful as

[9]"Delivery Costs," Postal Inspection Service, July 1988.

[10]Ibid., p. 9.

[11]John Crutcher, Commissioner of the Postal Rate Commission, remarks before the Winston-Salem, N.C., Rotary Club, May 9, 1989.

[12]OMB.

[13]OMB.

hoped. Many letters receiving the bar code discount are, in fact, sorted by hand because of current equipment inadequacies and shortages. Free of the institutionalized restrictions that encumber the USPS, the private sector would be better able to take advantage of the opportunities available through expanded use of high technologies.

If fully implemented, the above recommendations would yield savings that would more than offset the loss of the taxpayer subsidy now received each year by the USPS. They would also yield better service to the customers and limit the postal rate increases that are likely to occur within the next year or two. Even with the current $1.5 billion annual subsidy, the USPS will probably have to request an increase of $.05 or more in the price of a first class stamp in late 1990 or early 1991 as a result of worsening financial losses and projected employee pay increases. This year, for example, USPS payroll costs are running about $1 billion more than anticipated.[14]

In addition to granting the now financially independent USPS off-budget status, the administration might want to sweeten the offer by granting to USPS management the right to set its own rates for all those classes of mail where a competitive market currently exists, and to be subject to the review of the Rate Commission only in those classes where it maintains a monopoly under the private express statutes. Rate-setting independence in those classes—notably first and third class—would be attained when the USPS relinquishes its monopoly power in these lines of business, provided, however, that it can demonstrate that monopoly profits earned in any remaining lines are not used to subsidize unfair competition with private firms.

The USPS's campaign to remove itself from the federal budget and from the financial discipline of the congressional budget process poses a challenge and an opportunity to the president and Congress. Absent effective action, the current $1.5 billion taxpayer subsidy will rise to $2.5 billion by FY 1994, and postal rates will rise just as dramatically, as USPS costs continue to climb at a rapid rate. Simply moving the USPS off-budget would make it even less responsive to government oversight and customer needs.

[14]Crutcher.

About the Editor

Peter J. Ferrara is associate professor of law at the George Mason University School of Law and a senior fellow at the Cato Institute. He previously served as a senior staff member in the White House Office of Policy Development and as special assistant to the assistant secretary for policy development at the Department of Housing and Urban Development. He is the author of *Social Security: The Inherent Contradiction* and *Social Security: Averting the Crisis* and editor of *Social Security: Prospects for Real Reform*.

Cato Institute

Founded in 1977, the Cato Institute is a public policy research foundation dedicated to broadening the parameters of policy debate to allow consideration of more options that are consistent with the traditional American principles of limited government, individual liberty, and peace. Toward that goal, the Institute strives to achieve a greater involvement of the intelligent, concerned lay public in questions of policy and the proper role of government.

The Institute is named for *Cato's Letters*, pamphlets that were widely read in the American Colonies in the early 18th century and played a major role in laying the philosophical foundation for the revolution that followed. Since that revolution, civil and economic liberties have been eroded as the number and complexity of social problems have grown.

To counter this trend the Cato Institute undertakes an extensive publications program dealing with the complete spectrum of policy issues. Books, monographs, and shorter studies are commissioned to examine the federal budget, Social Security, regulation, NATO, international trade, and a myriad of other issues. Major policy conferences are held throughout the year, from which papers are published thrice yearly in the *Cato Journal*.

In order to maintain an independent posture, the Cato Institute accepts no government funding. Contributions are received from foundations, corporations, and individuals, and other revenue is generated from the sale of publications. The Institute is a nonprofit, tax-exempt, educational foundation under Section 501(c)3 of the Internal Revenue Code.

CATO INSTITUTE
224 Second St., S.E.
Washington, D.C. 20003